Mark Rutherford's Deliverance

Mark Rutherford

Contents

MARK RUTHERFORD'S DELIVERANCE

BY

Mark Rutherford

CHAPTER I--NEWSPAPERS

When I had established myself in my new lodgings in Camden Town, I found I had ten pounds in my pocket, and again there was no outlook. I examined carefully every possibility. At last I remembered that a relative of mine, who held some office in the House of Commons, added to his income by writing descriptive accounts of the debates, throwing in by way of supplement any stray scraps of gossip which he was enabled to collect. The rules of the House as to the admission of strangers were not so strict then as they are now, and he assured me that if I could but secure a commission from a newspaper, he could pass me into one of the galleries, and, when there was nothing to be heard worth describing, I could remain in the lobby, where I should by degrees find many opportunities of picking up intelligence which would pay. So far, so good; but how to obtain the commission? I managed to get hold of a list of all the country papers, and I wrote to nearly every one, offering my services. I am afraid that I somewhat exaggerated them, for I had two answers, and, after a little correspondence, two engagements. This was an unexpected stroke of luck; but alas! both journals circulated in the same district. I never could get together more stuff than would fill about a column and a half, and consequently I was obliged, with infinite pains, to vary, so that it could not be recognised, the form of what, at bottom, was essentially the same matter. This was work which would have been disagreeable enough, if I had not now ceased in a great measure to demand what was agreeable. In years past I coveted a life, not of mere sensual enjoyment--for that I never cared--but a life which should be filled with activities of the noblest kind, and it was intolerable to me to reflect that all my waking hours were in the main passed in merest drudgery, and that only for a few moments at the beginning or end of the day could it be said that the higher sympathies were really operative. Existence to me was nothing but these few moments, and consequently flitted like a shadow. I was now, however, the better of what was half disease and half something healthy and good. In the first place, I had discovered that my appetite was far larger than my powers. Consumed by a longing for continuous intercourse with the best, I had no ability whatever to maintain it, and I had accepted as a fact, however mysterious it might be, that the human mind is created with the impulses of a seraph and the strength of a man. Furthermore, what was I that I should demand exceptional treatment? Thousands of men and women superior to myself, are condemned, if that is the proper word to use, to almost total absence from themselves. The roar of the world for them is never lulled to rest, nor can silence ever be secured in which the voice of the Divine can be heard.

My letters were written twice a week, and as each contained a column and a half, I had six columns weekly to manufacture. These I was in the habit of writing in the morning, my evenings being spent at the House. At first I was rather interested, but after a while the occupation became tedious beyond measure, and for this reason. In a discussion of any importance about fifty members perhaps would take part, and had made up their minds beforehand to speak. There could not possibly be more than three or four reasons for or against the motion, and as the knowledge that what the intending orator had to urge had been urged a dozen times before on that very night never deterred him from urging it again, the same arguments, diluted, muddled, and mispresented, recurred with the most wearisome iteration.

The public outside knew nothing or very little of the real House of Commons, and the manner in which time was squandered there, for the reports were all of them much abbreviated. In fact, I doubt whether anybody but the Speaker, and one or two other persons in the same position as myself, really felt with proper intensity what the waste was, and how profound was the vanity of members and the itch for expression; for even the reporters were relieved at stated intervals, and the impression on their minds was not continuous. Another evil result of these attendances at the House was a kind of political scepticism. Over and over again I have seen a Government arraigned for its conduct of foreign affairs. The evidence lay in masses of correspondence which it would have required some days to master, and the verdict, after knowing the facts, ought to have depended upon the application of principles, each of which admitted a contrary principle for which much might be pleaded. There were not fifty members in the House with the leisure or the ability to understand what it was which had actually happened, and if they had understood it, they would not have had the wit to see what was the rule which ought to have decided the case. Yet, whether they understood or not, they were obliged to vote, and what was worse, the constituencies also had to vote, and so the gravest matters were settled in utter ignorance. This has often been adduced as an argument against an extended suffrage, but, if it is an argument against anything, it is an argument against intrusting the aristocracy and even the House itself with the destinies of the nation; for no dock labourer could possibly be more entirely empty of all reasons for action than the noble lords, squires, lawyers, and railway directors whom I have seen troop to the division bell. There is something deeper than this scepticism, but the scepticism is the easiest and the most obvious conclusion to an open mind dealing so closely and practically with politics as it was my lot to do at this time of my life. Men must be governed, and when it comes to the question, by whom? I, for one, would far sooner in the long run trust the people at large than I would the few, who in everything which relates to Government are as little instructed as the many and more difficult to move. The very fickleness of the multitude, the theme of such constant declamation, is so far good that it proves a susceptibility to impressions to which men hedged round by impregnable conventionalities cannot yield.[1]

When I was living in the country, the pure sky and the landscape formed a large portion of my existence, so large that much of myself depended on it, and I wondered how men could be worth anything if they could never see the face of nature. For this belief my early training on the "Lyrical Ballads" is answerable. When I came to London the same creed survived, and I was for ever thirsting for intercourse with my ancient friend. Hope, faith, and God seemed impossible amidst the smoke of the streets. It was now very difficult for me, except at rare opportunities, to leave London, and it was necessary for me, therefore, to understand that all that was essential for me was obtainable there, even though I should never see anything more than was to be seen in journeying through the High Street, Camden Town, Tottenham Court Road, the Seven Dials, and Whitehall. I should have been guilty of a simple surrender to despair if I had not forced myself to make this discovery.

1   This was written many years ago, but is curiously pertinent to the discussions of this year.-- EDITOR, 1884.

I cannot help saying, with all my love for the literature of my own day, that it has an evil side to it which none know except the millions of sensitive persons who are condemned to exist in great towns. It might be imagined from much of this literature that true humanity and a belief in God are the offspring of the hills or the ocean; and by implication, if not expressly, the vast multitudes who hardly ever see the hills or the ocean must be without a religion. The long poems which turn altogether upon scenery, perhaps in foreign lands, and the passionate devotion to it which they breathe, may perhaps do good in keeping alive in the hearts of men a determination to preserve air, earth, and water from pollution; but speaking from experience as a Londoner, I can testify that they are most depressing, and I would counsel everybody whose position is what mine was to avoid these books and to associate with those which will help him in his own circumstances.

Half of my occupation soon came to an end. One of my editors sent me a petulant note telling me that all I wrote he could easily find out himself, and that he required something more "graphic and personal." I could do no better, or rather I ought to say, no worse than I had been doing. These letters were a great trouble to me. I was always conscious of writing so much of which I was not certain, and so much which was indifferent to me. The unfairness of parties haunted me. But I continued to write, because I saw no other way of getting a living, and surely it is a baser dishonesty to depend upon the charity of friends because some pleasant, clean, ideal employment has not presented itself, than to soil one's hands with a little of the inevitable mud. I don't think I ever felt anything more keenly than I did a sneer from an acquaintance of mine who was in the habit of borrowing money from me. He was a painter, whose pictures were never sold because he never worked hard enough to know how to draw, and it came to my ears indirectly that he had said that "he would rather live the life of a medieval ascetic than condescend to the degradation of scribbling a dozen columns weekly of utter trash on subjects with which he had no concern." At that very moment he owed me five pounds. God knows that I admitted my dozen columns to be utter trash, but it ought to have been forgiven by those who saw that I was struggling to save myself from the streets and to keep a roof over my head. Degraded, however, as I might be, I could not get down to the "graphic and personal," for it meant nothing less than the absolutely false. I therefore contrived to exist on the one letter, which, excepting the mechanical labour of writing a second, took up as much of my time as if I had to write two.

Never, but once or twice at the most, did my labours meet with the slightest recognition beyond payment. Once I remember that I accused a member of a discreditable manoeuvre to consume the time of the House, and as he represented a borough in my district, he wrote to the editor denying the charge. The editor without any inquiry--and I believe I was mistaken--instantly congratulated me on having "scored." At another time, when Parliament was not sitting, I ventured, by way of filling up my allotted space, to say a word on behalf of a now utterly forgotten novel. I had a letter from the authoress thanking me, but alas! the illusion vanished. I was tempted by this one novel to look into others which I found she had written, and I discovered that they were altogether silly. The attraction of the one of which I thought so highly, was due not to any real merit which it possessed, but to something I had put into it. It was dead, but it had served as a wall to re-echo my own voice. Excepting these two occasions, I don't think that one solitary human being ever applauded or condemned one solitary word of which I was the author. All my friends knew where my contributions were to be found, but I never heard that they looked at them. They were never worth reading, and yet such complete silence was rather lonely. The tradesman who makes a good coat enjoys the satisfaction of having fitted and pleased his customer, and a bricklayer, if he be diligent, is rewarded by knowing that his master understands his value, but I never knew what it was to receive a single response. I wrote for an abstraction; and spoke to empty space. I cannot help claiming some pity and even respect for the class to which I belonged. I have heard them called all kinds of hard names, hacks, drudges, and something even more contemptible, but the injustice done to them is monstrous. Their wage is hardly earned; it is peculiarly precarious, depending altogether upon their health, and no matter how ill they may be they must maintain the liveliness of manner which is necessary to procure acceptance. I fell in with one poor fellow whose line was something like my own. I became acquainted with him through sitting side by side with him at the House. He lived in lodgings in Goodge Street, and occasionally I walked with him as far as the corner of Tottenham Court Road, where I caught the last omnibus northward. He wrote like me a "descriptive article" for the country, but he also wrote every now and then--a dignity to which I never attained--a "special" for London. His "descriptive articles" were more political than mine, and he was obliged to be violently Tory. His creed, however, was such a pure piece of professionalism, that though I was Radical, and was expected to be so, we never jarred, and often, as we wandered homewards, we exchanged notes, and were mutually useful, his observations appearing in my paper, and mine in his, with proper modifications. How he used to roar in the Gazette against the opposite party, and yet I never heard anything from him myself but what was diffident and tender. He had acquired, as an instrument necessary to him, an extraordinarily extravagant style, and he laid about him with a bludgeon, which inevitably descended on the heads of all prominent persons if they happened not to be Conservative, no matter what their virtues might be. One peculiarity, however, I noted in him. Although he ought every now and then, when the subject was uppermost, to have flamed out in the Gazette on behalf of the Church, I never saw a word from him on that subject. He drew the line at religion. He did not mind acting his part in things secular, for his performances were, I am sure, mostly histrionic, but there he stopped. The unreality of his character was a husk surrounding him, but it did not touch the core. It was as if he had said to himself, "Political controversy is nothing to me, and, what is more, is so uncertain that it matters little whether I say yes or no, nor indeed does it matter if I say yes AND no, and I must keep my wife and children from the workhouse; but when it comes to the relationship of man to God, it is a different matter." His altogether outside vehemence and hypocrisy did in fact react upon him, and so far from affecting harmfully what lay deeper, produced a more complete sincerity and transparency extending even to the finest verbal distinctions. Over and over again have I heard him preach to his wife, almost with pathos, the duty of perfect exactitude in speech in describing the commonest occurrences. "Now, my dear, IS that so?" was a perpetual remonstrance with him; and he always insisted upon it that there is no training more necessary for children than that of teaching them not merely to speak the truth in the ordinary, vulgar sense of the term, but to speak it in a much higher sense, by rigidly compelling, point by point, a correspondence of the words with the fact external or internal. He never would tolerate in his own children a mere hackneyed, borrowed expression, but demanded exact portraiture; and nothing vexed him more than to hear one of them spoil and make worthless what he or she had seen, by reporting it in some stale phrase which had been used by everybody. This refusal to take the trouble to watch the presentment to the mind of anything which had been placed before it, and to reproduce it in its own lines and colours was, as he said, nothing but falsehood, and he maintained that the principal reason why people are so uninteresting is not that they have nothing to say. It is rather that they will not face the labour of saying in their own tongue what they have to say, but cover it up and conceal it in commonplace, so that we get, not what they themselves behold and what they think, but a hieroglyphic or symbol invented as the representative of a certain class of objects or emotions, and as inefficient to represent a particular object or emotion as x or y to set forth the relation of Hamlet to Ophelia. He would even exercise his children in this art of the higher truthfulness, and would purposely make them give him an account of something which he had seen and they had seen, checking them the moment he saw a lapse from originality. Such was the Tory correspondent of the Gazette.

I ought to say, by way of apology for him, that in his day it signified little or nothing whether Tory or Whig was in power. Politics had not become what they will one day become, a matter of life or death, dividing men with really private love and hate. What a mockery controversy was in the House! How often I have seen members, who were furious at one another across the floor, quietly shaking hands outside, and inviting one another to dinner! I have heard them say that we ought to congratulate ourselves that parliamentary differences do not in this country breed personal animosities. To me this seemed anything but a subject of congratulation. Men who are totally at variance ought not to be friends, and if Radical and Tory are not totally, but merely superficially at variance, so much the worse for their Radicalism and Toryism.

It is possible, and even probable, that the public fury and the subsequent amity were equally absurd. Most of us have no real loves and no real hatreds. Blessed is love, less blessed is hatred, but thrice accursed is that indifference which is neither one nor the other, the muddy mess which men call friendship.

M'Kay--for that was his name--lived, as I have said, in Goodge Street, where he had unfurnished apartments. I often spent part of the Sunday with him, and I may forestall obvious criticism by saying that I do not pretend for a moment to defend myself from inconsistency in denouncing members of Parliament for their duplicity, M'Kay and myself being also guilty of something very much like it. But there was this difference between us and our parliamentary friends, that we always divested ourselves of all hypocrisy when we were alone. We then dropped the stage costume which members continued to wear in the streets and at the dinner- table, and in which some of them even slept and said their prayers.

London Sundays to persons who are not attached to any religious community, and have no money to spend, are rather dreary. We tried several ways of getting through the morning. If we heard that there was a preacher with a reputation, we went to hear him. As a rule, however, we got no good in that way. Once we came to a chapel where there was a minister supposed to be one of the greatest orators of the day. We had much difficulty in finding standing room. Just as we entered we heard him say, "My friends, I appeal to those of you who are parents. You know that if you say to a child 'go,' he goeth, and if you say 'come,' he cometh. So the Lord"--But at this point M'Kay, who had children, nudged me to come out; and out we went. Why does this little scene remain with me? I can hardly say, but here it stands. It is remembered, not so much by reason of the preacher as by reason of the apparent acquiescence and admiration of the audience, who seemed to be perfectly willing to take over an experience from their pastor--if indeed it was really an experience-- which was not their own. Our usual haunts on Sunday were naturally the parks and Kensington Gardens; but artificial limited enclosures are apt to become wearisome after a time, and we longed for a little more freedom if a little less trim. So we would stroll towards Hampstead or Highgate, the only drawback to these regions being the squalid, ragged, half town, half suburb, through which it was necessary to pass. The skirts of London when the air is filled with north-easterly soot, grit, and filth, are cheerless, and the least cheerful part of the scene is the inability of the vast wandering masses of people to find any way of amusing themselves. At the corner of one of the fields in Kentish Town, just about to be devoured, stood a public-house, and opposite the door was generally encamped a man who sold nothing but Brazil nuts. Swarms of people lazily wandered past him, most of them waiting for the public-house to open. Brazil nuts on a cold black Sunday morning are not exhilarating, but the costermonger found many customers who bought his nuts, and ate them, merely because they had nothing better to do. We went two or three times to a freethinking hall, where we were entertained with demonstrations of the immorality of the patriarchs and Jewish heroes, and arguments to prove that the personal existence of the devil was a myth, the audience breaking out into uproarious laughter at comical delineations of Noah and Jonah. One morning we found the place completely packed. A "celebrated Christian," as he was described to us, having heard of the hall, had volunteered to engage in debate on the claims of the Old Testament to Divine authority. He turned out to be a preacher whom we knew quite well. He was introduced by his freethinking antagonist, who claimed for him a respectful hearing. The preacher said that before beginning he should like to "engage in prayer." Accordingly he came to the front of the platform, lifted up his eyes, told God why he was there, and besought Him to bless the discussion in the conversion "of these poor wandering souls, who have said in their hearts that there is no God, to a saving faith in Him and in the blood of Christ." I expected that some resentment would be displayed when the wandering souls found themselves treated like errant sheep, but to my surprise they listened with perfect silence; and when he had said "Amen," there were great clappings of hands, and cries of "Bravo." They evidently considered the prayer merely as an elocutionary show-piece. The preacher was much disconcerted, but he recovered himself, and began his sermon, for it was nothing more. He enlarged on the fact that men of the highest eminence had believed in the Old Testament. Locke and Newton had believed in it, and did it not prove arrogance in us to doubt when the "gigantic intellect which had swept the skies, and had announced the law which bound the universe together was satisfied?" The witness of the Old Testament to the New was another argument, but his main reliance was upon the prophecies. From Adam to Isaiah there was a continuous prefigurement of Christ. Christ was the point to which everything tended; and "now, my friends," he said, "I cannot sit down without imploring you to turn your eyes on Him who never yet repelled the sinner, to wash in that eternal Fountain ever open for the remission of sins, and to flee from the wrath to come. I believe the sacred symbol of the cross has not yet lost its efficacy. For eighteen hundred years, whenever it has been exhibited to the sons of men, it has been potent to reclaim and save them. 'I, if I be lifted up,' cried the Great Sufferer, 'will draw all men unto Me,' and He has drawn not merely the poor and ignorant but the philosopher and the sage. Oh, my brethren, think what will happen if you reject Him. I forbear to paint your doom. And think again, on the other hand, of the bliss which awaits you if you receive Him, of the eternal companionship with the Most High and with the spirits of just men made perfect." His hearers again applauded vigorously, and none less so than their appointed leader, who was to follow on the other side. He was a little man with small eyes; his shaven face was dark with a black beard lurking under the skin, and his nose was slightly turned up. He was evidently a trained debater who had practised under railway arches, discussion "forums," and in the classes promoted by his sect. He began by saying that he could not compliment his friend who had just sat down on the inducements which he had offered them to become Christians. The New Cut was not a nice place on a wet day, but he had rather sit at a stall there all day long with his feet on a basket than lie in the bosom of some of the just men made perfect portrayed in the Bible. Nor, being married, should he feel particularly at ease if he had to leave his wife with David. David certainly ought to have got beyond all that kind of thing, considering it must be over 3000 years since he first saw Bathsheba; but we are told that the saints are for ever young in heaven, and this treacherous villain, who would have been tried by a jury of twelve men and hung outside Newgate if he had lived in the nineteenth century, might be dangerous now. He was an amorous old gentleman up to the very last. (Roars of laughter.) Nor did the speaker feel particularly anxious to be shut up with all the bishops, who of course are amongst the elect, and on their departure from this vale of tears tempered by ten thousand a year, are duly supplied with wings. Much more followed in the same strain upon the immorality of the Bible heroes, their cruelty, and the cruelty of the God who sanctioned it. Then followed a clever exposition of the inconsistencies of the Old Testament history, the impossibility of any reference to Jesus therein, and a really earnest protest against the quibbling by which those who believed in the Bible as a revelation sought to reconcile it with science. "Finally," said the speaker, "I am sure we all of us will pass a vote of thanks to our reverend friend for coming to see us, and we cordially invite him to come again. If I might be allowed to offer a suggestion, it would be that he should make himself acquainted with our case before he pays us another visit, and not suppose that we are to be persuaded with the rhetoric which may do very well for the young women of his congregation, but won't go down here." This was fair and just, for the eminent Christian was nothing but an ordinary minister, who, when he was prepared for his profession, had never been allowed to see what are the historical difficulties of Christianity, lest he should be overcome by them. On the other hand, his sceptical opponents were almost devoid of the faculty for appreciating the great remains of antiquity, and would probably have considered the machinery of the Prometheus Bound or of the Iliad a sufficient reason for a sneer. That they should spend their time in picking the Bible to pieces when there was so much positive work for them to do, seemed to me as melancholy as if they had spent themselves upon theology. To waste a Sunday morning in ridiculing such stories as that of Jonah was surely as imbecile as to waste it in proving their verbal veracity.

CHAPTER II--M'KAY

It was foggy and overcast as we walked home to Goodge Street. The churches and chapels were emptying themselves, but the great mass of the population had been "nowhere." I had dinner with M'Kay, and as the day wore on the fog thickened. London on a dark Sunday afternoon, more especially about Goodge Street, is depressing. The inhabitants drag themselves hither and thither in languor and uncertainty. Small mobs loiter at the doors of the gin palaces. Costermongers wander aimlessly, calling "walnuts" with a cry so melancholy that it sounds as the wail of the hopelessly lost may be imagined to sound when their anguish has been deadened by the monotony of a million years.

About two or three o'clock decent working men in their best clothes emerge from the houses in such streets as Nassau Street. It is part of their duty to go out after dinner on Sunday with the wife and children. The husband pushes the per-ambulator out of the dingy passage, and gazes doubtfully this way and that way, not knowing whither to go, and evidently longing for the Monday, when his work, however disagreeable it may be, will be his plain duty. The wife follows carrying a child, and a boy and girl in unaccustomed apparel walk by her side. They come out into Mortimer Street. There are no shops open; the sky over their heads is mud, the earth is mud under their feet, the muddy houses stretch in long rows, black, gaunt, uniform. The little party reach Hyde Park, also wrapped in impenetrable mud-grey. The man's face brightens for a moment as he says, "It is time to go back," and so they return, without the interchange of a word, unless perhaps they happen to see an omnibus horse fall down on the greasy stones. What is there worth thought or speech on such an expedition? Nothing! The tradesman who kept the oil and colour establishment opposite to us was not to be tempted outside. It was a little more comfortable than Nassau Street, and, moreover, he was religious and did not encourage Sabbath-breaking. He and his family always moved after their mid-day Sabbath repast from the little back room behind the shop up to what they called the drawing-room overhead. It was impossible to avoid seeing them every time we went to the window. The father of the family, after his heavy meal, invariably sat in the easy-chair with a handkerchief over his eyes and slept. The children were always at the windows, pretending to read books, but in reality watching the people below. At about four o'clock their papa generally awoke, and demanded a succession of hymn tunes played on the piano. When the weather permitted, the lower sash was opened a little, and the neighbours were indulged with the performance of "Vital Spark," the father "coming in" now and then with a bass note or two at the end where he was tolerably certain of the harmony. At five o'clock a prophecy of the incoming tea brought us some relief from the contemplation of the landscape or brick-scape. I say "some relief," for meals at M'Kay's were a little disagreeable. His wife was an honest, good little woman, but so much attached to him and so dependent on him that she was his mere echo. She had no opinions which were not his, and whenever he said anything which went beyond the ordinary affairs of the house, she listened with curious effort, and generally responded by a weakened repetition of M'Kay's own observations. He perpetually, therefore, had before him an enfeebled reflection of himself, and this much irritated him, notwithstanding his love for her; for who could help loving a woman who, without the least hesitation, would have opened her veins at his command, and have given up every drop of blood in her body for him? Over and over again I have heard him offer some criticism on a person or event, and the customary chime of approval would ensue, provoking him to such a degree that he would instantly contradict himself with much bitterness, leaving poor Mrs. M'Kay in much perplexity. Such a shot as this generally reduced her to timid silence. As a rule, he always discouraged any topic at his house which was likely to serve as an occasion for showing his wife's dependence on him. He designedly talked about her household affairs, asked her whether she had mended his clothes and ordered the coals. She knew that these things were not what was upon his mind, and she answered him in despairing tones, which showed how much she felt the obtrusive condescension to her level. I greatly pitied her, and sometimes, in fact, my emotion at the sight of her struggles with her limitations almost overcame me and I was obliged to get up and go. She was childishly affectionate. If M'Kay came in and happened to go up to her and kiss her, her face brightened into the sweetest and happiest smile. I recollect once after he had been unusually annoyed with her he repented just as he was leaving home, and put his lips to her head, holding it in both his hands. I saw her gently take the hand from her forehead and press it to her mouth, the tears falling down her cheek meanwhile. Nothing would ever tempt her to admit anything against her husband. M'Kay was violent and unjust at times. His occupation he hated, and his restless repugnance to it frequently discharged itself indifferently upon everything which came in his way. His children often thought him almost barbarous, but in truth he did not actually see them when he was in one of these moods. What was really present with him, excluding everything else, was the sting of something more than usually repulsive of which they knew nothing. Mrs. M'Kay's answer to her children's remonstrances when they were alone with her always was, "He is so worried," and she invariably dwelt upon their faults which had given him the opportunity for his wrath.

I think M'Kay's treatment of her wholly wrong. I think that he ought not to have imposed himself upon her so imperiously. I think he ought to have striven to ascertain what lay concealed in that modest heart, to have encouraged its expression and development, to have debased himself before her that she might receive courage to rise, and he would have found that she had something which he had not; not HIS something perhaps, but something which would have made his life happier. As it was, he stood upon his own ground above her. If she could reach him, well and good, if not, the helping hand was not proffered, and she fell back, hopeless. Later on he discovered his mistake. She became ill very gradually, and M'Kay began to see in the distance a prospect of losing her. A frightful pit came in view. He became aware that he could not do without her. He imagined what his home would have been with other women whom he knew, and he confessed that with them he would have been less contented. He acknowledged that he had been guilty of a kind of criminal epicurism; that he rejected in foolish, fatal, nay, even wicked indifference, the bread of life upon which he might have lived and thrived. His whole effort now was to suppress himself in his wife. He read to her, a thing he never did before, and when she misunderstood, he patiently explained; he took her into his counsels and asked her opinion; he abandoned his own opinion for hers, and in the presence of her children he always deferred to her, and delighted to acknowledge that she knew more than he did, that she was right and he was wrong. She was now confined to her house, and the end was near, but this was the most blessed time of her married life. She grew under the soft rain of his loving care, and opened out, not, indeed, into an oriental flower, rich in profound mystery of scent and colour, but into a blossom of the chalk-down. Altogether concealed and closed she would have remained if it had not been for this beneficent and heavenly gift poured upon her. He had just time enough to see what she really was, and then she died. There are some natures that cannot unfold under pressure or in the presence of unregarding power. Hers was one. They require a clear space round them, the removal of everything which may overmaster them, and constant delicate attention. They require too a recognition of the fact, which M'Kay for a long time did not recognise, that it is folly to force them and to demand of them that they shall be what they cannot be. I stood by the grave this morning of my poor, pale, clinging little friend now for some years at peace, and I thought that the tragedy of Promethean torture or Christ-like crucifixion may indeed be tremendous, but there is a tragedy too in the existence of a soul like hers, conscious of its feebleness and ever striving to overpass it, ever aware that it is an obstacle to the return of the affection of the man whom she loves.

Meals, as I have said, were disagreeable at M'Kay's, and when we wanted to talk we went out of doors. The evening after our visit to the debating hall we moved towards Portland Place, and walked up and down there for an hour or more. M'Kay had a passionate desire to reform the world. The spectacle of the misery of London, and of the distracted swaying hither and thither of the multitudes who inhabit it, tormented him incessantly. He always chafed at it, and he never seemed sure that he had a right to the enjoyment of the simplest pleasures so long as London was before him. What a farce, he would cry, is all this poetry, philosophy, art, and culture, when millions of wretched mortals are doomed to the eternal darkness and crime of the city! Here are the educated classes occupying themselves with exquisite emotions, with speculations upon the Infinite, with addresses to flowers, with the worship of waterfalls and flying clouds, and with the incessant portraiture of a thousand moods and variations of love, while their neighbours lie grovelling in the mire, and never know anything more of life or its duties than is afforded them by a police report in a bit of newspaper picked out of the kennel. We went one evening to hear a great violin-player, who played such music, and so exquisitely, that the limits of life were removed. But we had to walk up the Haymarket home, between eleven and twelve o'clock, and the violin-playing became the merest trifling. M'Kay had been brought up upon the Bible. He had before him, not only there, but in the history of all great religious movements, a record of the improvement of the human race, or of large portions of it, not merely by gradual civilisation, but by inspiration spreading itself suddenly. He could not get it out of his head that something of this kind is possible again in our time. He longed to try for himself in his own poor way in one of the slums about Drury Lane. I sympathised with him, but I asked him what he had to say. I remember telling him that I had been into St. Paul's Cathedral, and that I pictured to myself the cathedral full, and myself in the pulpit. I was excited while imagining the opportunity offered me of delivering some message to three or four thousand persons in such a building, but in a minute or two I discovered that my sermon would be very nearly as follows: "Dear friends, I know no more than you know; we had better go home." I admitted to him that if he could believe in hell-fire, or if he could proclaim the Second Advent, as Paul did to the Thessalonians, and get people to believe, he might change their manners, but otherwise he could do nothing but resort to a much slower process. With the departure of a belief in the supernatural departs once and for ever the chance of regenerating the race except by the school and by science.[2] However, M'Kay thought he would try. His earnestness was rather a hindrance than a help to him, for it prevented his putting certain important questions to himself, or at any rate it prevented his waiting for distinct answers. He recurred to the apostles and Bunyan, and was convinced that it was possible even now to touch depraved men and women with an idea which should recast their lives. So it is that the main obstacle to our success is a success which has preceded us. We instinctively follow the antecedent form, and consequently we either pass by, or deny altogether, the life of our own time, because its expression has changed. We never do practically believe that the Messiah is not incarnated twice in the same flesh. He came as Jesus, and we look for Him as Jesus now, overlooking the manifestation of to-day, and dying,

---

2 Not exactly untrue, but it sounds strangely now when socialism, nationalisation of the land, and other projects have renewed in men the hope of regeneration by political processes. The reader will, however, please remember the date of these memoirs.--EDITOR, 1884.

perhaps, without recognising it.

M'Kay had found a room near Parker Street, Drury Lane, in which he proposed to begin, and that night, as we trod the pavement of Portland Place, he propounded his plans to me, I listening without much confidence, but loth nevertheless to take the office of Time upon myself, and to disprove what experience would disprove more effectually. His object was nothing less than gradually to attract Drury Lane to come and be saved.

The first Sunday I went with him to the room. As we walked over the Drury Lane gratings of the cellars a most foul stench came up, and one in particular I remember to this day. A man half dressed pushed open a broken window beneath us, just as we passed by, and there issued such a blast of corruption, made up of gases bred by filth, air breathed and rebreathed a hundred times, charged with odours of unnameable personal uncleanness and disease, that I staggered to the gutter with a qualm which I could scarcely conquer. At the doors of the houses stood grimy women with their arms folded and their hair disordered. Grimier boys and girls had tied a rope to broken railings, and were swinging on it. The common door to a score of lodgings stood ever open, and the children swarmed up and down the stairs carrying with them patches of mud every time they came in from the street. The wholesome practice which amongst the decent poor marks off at least one day in the week as a day on which there is to be a change; when there is to be some attempt to procure order and cleanliness; a day to be preceded by soap and water, by shaving, and by as many clean clothes as can be procured, was unknown here. There was no break in the uniformity of squalor; nor was it even possible for any single family to emerge amidst such altogether suppressive surroundings. All self-respect, all effort to do anything more than to satisfy somehow the grossest wants, had departed. The shops were open; most of them exhibiting a most miscellaneous collection of goods, such as bacon cut in slices, fire-wood, a few loaves of bread, and sweetmeats in dirty bottles. Fowls, strange to say, black as the flagstones, walked in and out of these shops, or descended into the dark areas. The undertaker had not put up his shutters. He had drawn down a yellow blind, on which was painted a picture of a suburban cemetery. Two funerals, the loftiest effort of his craft, were depicted approaching the gates. When the gas was alight behind the blind, an effect was produced which was doubtless much admired. He also displayed in his window a model coffin, a work of art. It was about a foot long, varnished, studded with little brass nails, and on the lid was fastened a rustic cross stretching from end to end. The desire to decorate existence in some way or other with more or less care is nearly universal. The most sensual and the meanest almost always manifest an indisposition to be content with mere material satisfaction. I have known selfish, gluttonous, drunken men spend their leisure moments in trimming a bed of scarlet geraniums, and the vulgarest and most commonplace of mortals considers it a necessity to put a picture in the room or an ornament on the mantelpiece. The instinct, even in its lowest forms, is divine. It is the commentary on the text that man shall not live by bread alone. It is evidence of an acknowledged compulsion--of which art is the highest manifestation--to ESCAPE. In the alleys behind Drury Lane this instinct, the very salt of life, was dead, crushed out utterly, a symptom which seemed to me ominous, and even awful to the last degree. The only house in which it survived was in that of the undertaker, who displayed the willows, the black horses, and the coffin. These may have been nothing more than an advertisement, but from the care with which the cross was elaborated, and the neatness with which it was made to resemble a natural piece of wood, I am inclined to believe that the man felt some pleasure in his work for its own sake, and that he was not utterly submerged. The cross in such dens as these, or, worse than dens, in such sewers! If it be anything, it is a symbol of victory, of power to triumph over resistance, and even death. Here was nothing but sullen subjugation, the most grovelling slavery, mitigated only by a tendency to mutiny. Here was a strength of circumstance to quell and dominate which neither Jesus nor Paul could have overcome--worse a thousandfold than Scribes or Pharisees, or any form of persecution. The preaching of Jesus would have been powerless here; in fact, no known stimulus, nothing ever held up before men to stir the soul to activity, can do anything in the back streets of great cities so long as they are the cesspools which they are now.

We came to the room. About a score of M'Kay's own friends were there, and perhaps half-a-dozen outsiders, attracted by the notice which had been pasted on a board at the entrance. M'Kay announced his errand. The ignorance and misery of London he said were intolerable to him. He could not take any pleasure in life when he thought upon them. What could he do? that was the question. He was not a man of wealth. He could not buy up these hovels. He could not force an entrance into them and persuade their inhabitants to improve themselves. He had no talents wherewith to found a great organisation or create public opinion. He had determined, after much thought, to do what he was now doing. It was very little, but it was all he could undertake. He proposed to keep this room open as a place to which those who wished might resort at different times, and find some quietude, instruction, and what fortifying thoughts he could collect to enable men to endure their almost unendurable sufferings. He did not intend to teach theology. Anything which would be serviceable he would set forth, but in the main he intended to rely on holding up the examples of those who were greater than ourselves and were our redeemers. He meant to teach Christ in the proper sense of the word. Christ now is admired probably more than He had ever been. Everybody agrees to admire Him, but where are the people who really do what He did? There is no religion now-a-days. Religion is a mere literature. Cultivated persons sit in their studies and write overflowingly about Jesus, or meet at parties and talk about Him; but He is not of much use to me unless I say to myself, HOW IS IT WITH THEE? unless I myself become what He was. This was the meaning of Jesus to the Apostle Paul. Jesus was in him; he had put on Jesus; that is to say, Jesus lived in him like a second soul, taking the place of his own soul and directing him accordingly. That was religion, and it is absurd to say that the English nation at this moment, or any section of it, is religious. Its educated classes are inhabited by a hundred minds. We are in a state of anarchy, each of us with a different aim and shaping himself according to a different type; while the uneducated classes are entirely given over to the "natural man." He was firmly persuaded that we need religion, poor and rich alike. We need some controlling influence to bind together our scattered energies. We do not know what we are doing. We read one book one day and another book another day, but it is idle wandering to right and left; it is not advancing on a straight road. It is not possible to bind ourselves down to a certain defined course, but still it is an enormous, an incalculable advantage for us to have some irreversible standard set up in us by which everything we meet is to be judged. That is the meaning of the prophecy--whether it will ever be fulfilled God only knows--that Christ shall judge the world. All religions have been this. They have said that in the midst of the infinitely possible--infinitely possible evil and infinitely possible good too--we become distracted. A thousand forces good and bad act upon us. It is necessary, if we are to be men, if we are to be saved, that we should be rescued from this tumult, and that our feet should be planted upon a path. His object, therefore, would be to preach Christ, as before said, and to introduce into human life His unifying influence. He would try and get them to see things with the eyes of Christ, to love with His love, to judge with His judgment. He believed Christ was fitted to occupy this place. He deliberately chose Christ as worthy to be our central, shaping force. He would try by degrees to prove this; to prove that Christ's way of dealing with life is the best way, and so to create a genuinely Christian spirit, which, when any choice of conduct is presented to us, will prompt us to ask first of all, HOW WOULD CHRIST HAVE IT? or, when men and things pass before us, will decide through him what we have to say about them. M'Kay added that he hoped his efforts would not be confined to talking. He trusted to be able, by means of this little meeting, gradually to gain admittance for himself and his friends into the houses of the poor and do some practical good. At present he had no organisation and no plans. He did not believe in organisation and plans preceding a clear conception of what was to be accomplished. Such, as nearly as I can now recollect, is an outline of his discourse. It was thoroughly characteristic of him. He always talked in this fashion. He was for ever insisting on the aimlessness of modern life, on the powerlessness of its vague activities to mould men into anything good, to restrain them from evil or moderate their passions, and he was possessed by a vision of a new Christianity which was to take the place of the old and dead theologies. I have reported him in my own language. He strove as much as he could to make his meaning plain to everybody. Just before he finished, three or four out of the half-a- dozen outsiders who were present whistled with all their might and ran down the stairs shouting to one another. As we went out they had collected about the door, and amused themselves by pushing one another against us, and kicking an old kettle behind us and amongst us all the way up the street, so that we were covered with splashes. Mrs. M'Kay went with us, and when we reached home, she tried to say something about what she had heard. The cloud came over her husband's face at once; he remained silent for a minute, and getting up and going to the window, observed that it ought to be cleaned, and that he could hardly see the opposite house. The poor woman looked distressed, and I was just about to come to her rescue by continuing what she had been saying, when she rose, not in anger, but in trouble, and went upstairs.

CHAPTER III--MISS LEROY

During the great French war there were many French prisoners in my native town. They led a strange isolated life, for they knew nothing of our language, nor, in those days, did three people in the town understand theirs. The common soldiers amused themselves by making little trifles and selling them. I have now before me a box of coloured straw with the date 1799 on the bottom, which was bought by my grandfather. One of these prisoners was an officer named Leroy. Why he did not go back to France I never heard, but I know that before I was born he was living near our house on a small income; that he tried to teach French, and that he had as his companion a handsome daughter who grew up speaking English. What she was like when she was young I cannot say, but I have had her described to me over and over again. She had rather darkish brown hair, and she was tall and straight as an arrow. This she was, by the way, even into old age. She surprised, shocked, and attracted all the sober persons in our circle. Her ways were not their ways. She would walk out by herself on a starry night without a single companion, and cause thereby infinite talk, which would have converged to a single focus if it had not happened that she was also in the habit of walking out at four o'clock on a summer's morning, and that in the church porch of a little village not far from us, which was her favourite resting- place, a copy of the De Imitatione Christi was found which belonged to her. So the talk was scattered again and its convergence prevented. She used to say doubtful things about love. One of them struck my mother with horror. Miss Leroy told a male person once, and told him to his face, that if she loved him and he loved her, and they agreed to sign one another's foreheads with a cross as a ceremony, it would be as good to her as marriage. This may seem a trifle, but nobody now can imagine what was thought of it at the time it was spoken. My mother repeated it every now and then for fifty years. It may be conjectured how easily any other girls of our acquaintance would have been classified, and justly classified, if they had uttered such barefaced Continental immorality. Miss Leroy's neighbours were remarkably apt at classifying their fellow-creatures. They had a few, a very few holes, into which they dropped their neighbours, and they must go into one or the other. Nothing was more distressing than a specimen which, notwithstanding all the violence which might be used to it, would not fit into a hole, but remained an exception. Some lout, I believe, reckoning on the legitimacy of his generalisation, and having heard of this and other observations accredited to Miss Leroy, ventured to be slightly rude to her. What she said to him was never known, but he was always shy afterwards of mentioning her name, and when he did he was wont to declare that she was "a rum un." She was not particular, I have heard, about personal tidiness, and this I can well believe, for she was certainly not distinguished when I knew her for this virtue. She cared nothing for the linen-closet, the spotless bed-hangings, and the bright poker, which were the true household gods of the respectable women of those days. She would have been instantly set down as "slut," and as having "nasty dirty forrin ways," if a peculiar habit of hers had not unfortunately presented itself, most irritating to her critics, so anxious promptly to gratify their philosophic tendency towards scientific grouping. Mrs. Mobbs, who lived next door to her, averred that she always slept with the window open. Mrs. Mobbs, like everybody else, never opened her window except to "air the room." Mrs. Mobbs' best bedroom was carpeted all over, and contained a great four-post bedstead, hung round with heavy hangings, and protected at the top from draughts by a kind of firmament of white dimity. Mrs. Mobbs stuffed a sack of straw up the chimney of the fireplace, to prevent the fall of the "sutt," as she called it. Mrs. Mobbs, if she had a visitor, gave her a hot supper, and expected her immediately afterwards to go upstairs, draw the window curtains, get into this bed, draw the bed curtains also, and wake up the next morning "bilious." This was the proper thing to do. Miss Leroy's sitting- room was decidedly disorderly; the chairs were dusty; "yer might write yer name on the table," Mrs. Mobbs declared; but, nevertheless, the casement was never closed night nor day; and, moreover, Miss Leroy was believed by the strongest circumstantial evidence to wash herself all over every morning, a habit which Mrs. Mobbs thought "weakening," and somehow connected with ethical impropriety.

When Miss Leroy was married, and first as an elderly woman became known to me, she was very inconsequential in her opinions, or at least appeared so to our eyes. She must have been much more so when she was younger. In our town we were all formed upon recognised patterns, and those who possessed any one mark of the pattern, had all. The wine-merchant, for example, who went to church, eminently respectable, Tory, by no means associating with the tradesfolk who displayed their goods in the windows, knowing no "experience," and who had never felt the outpouring of the Spirit, was a specimen of a class like him. Another class was represented by the dissenting ironmonger, deacon, presiding at prayer-meetings, strict Sabbatarian, and believer in eternal punishments; while a third was set forth by "Guffy," whose real name was unknown, who got drunk, unloaded barges, assisted at the municipal elections, and was never once seen inside a place of worship. These patterns had existed amongst us from the dimmest antiquity, and were accepted as part of the eternal order of things; so much so, that the deacon, although he professed to be sure that nobody who had not been converted would escape the fire-- and the wine-merchant certainly had not been converted--was very far from admitting to himself that the wine-merchant ought to be converted, or that it would be proper to try and convert him. I doubt, indeed, whether our congregation would have been happy, or would have thought any the better of him, if he had left the church. Such an event, however, could no more come within the reach of our vision than a reversal of the current of our river. It would have broken up our foundations and party-walls, and would have been considered as ominous, and anything but a subject for thankfulness. But Miss Leroy was not the wine-merchant, nor the ironmonger, nor Guffy, and even now I cannot trace the hidden centre of union from which sprang so much that was apparently irreconcilable. She was a person whom nobody could have created in writing a novel, because she was so inconsistent. As I have said before, she studied Thomas a Kempis, and her little French Bible was brown with constant use. But then she read much fiction in which there were scenes which would have made our hair stand on end. The only thing she constantly abhorred in books was what was dull and opaque. Yet, as we shall see presently, her dislike to dulness, once at least in her life, notably failed her. She was not Catholic, and professed herself Protestant, but such a Protestantism! She had no sceptical doubts. She believed implicitly that the Bible was the Word of God, and that everything in it was true, but her interpretation of it was of the strangest kind. Almost all our great doctrines seemed shrunk to nothing in her eyes, while others, which were nothing to us, were all-important to her. The atonement, for instance, I never heard her mention, but Unitarianism was hateful to her, and Jesus was her God in every sense of the word. On the other hand, she was partly Pagan, for she knew very little of that consideration for the feeble, and even for the foolish, which is the glory of Christianity. She was rude to foolish people, and she instinctively kept out of the way of all disease and weakness, so that in this respect she was far below the commonplace tradesman's wife, who visited the sick, sat up with them, and, in fact, never seemed so completely in her element as when she could be with anybody who was ill in bed.

Miss Leroy's father was republican, and so was my grandfather. My grandfather and old Leroy were the only people in our town who refused to illuminate when a victory was gained over the French. Leroy's windows were spared on the ground that he was not a Briton, but the mob endeavoured to show my grandfather the folly of his belief in democracy by smashing every pane of glass in front of his house with stones. This drew him and Leroy together, and the result was, that although Leroy himself never set foot inside any chapel or church, Miss Leroy was often induced to attend our meeting-house in company with a maiden aunt of mine, who rather "took to her." Now comes the for ever mysterious passage in history. There was amongst the attendants at that meeting-house a young man who was apprentice to a miller. He was a big, soft, quiet, plump-faced, awkward youth, very good, but nothing more. He wore on Sunday a complete suit of light pepper-and-salt clothes, and continued to wear pepper-and-salt on Sunday all his life. He taught in the Sunday-school, and afterwards, as he got older, he was encouraged to open his lips at a prayer-meeting, and to "take the service" in the village chapels on Sunday evening. He was the most singularly placid, even-tempered person I ever knew. I first became acquainted with him when I was a child and he was past middle life. What he was then, I am told, he always was; and I certainly never heard one single violent word escape his lips. His habits, even when young, had a tendency to harden. He went to sleep after his mid-day dinner with the greatest regularity, and he never could keep awake if he sat by a fire after dark. I have seen him, when kneeling at family worship and praying with his family, lose himself for an instant and nod his head, to the confusion of all who were around him. He is dead now, but he lived to a good old age, which crept upon him gradually with no pain, and he passed away from this world to the next in a peaceful doze. He never read anything, for the simple reason that whenever he was not at work or at chapel he slumbered. To the utter amazement of everybody, it was announced one fine day that Miss Leroy and he-- George Butts--were to be married. They were about the last people in the world, who, it was thought, could be brought together. My mother was stunned, and never completely recovered. I have seen her, forty years after George Butts' wedding-day, lift up her hands, and have heard her call out with emotion, as fresh as if the event were of yesterday, "What made that girl have George I can NOT think--but there!" What she meant by the last two words we could not comprehend. Many of her acquaintances interpreted them to mean that she knew more than she dared communicate, but I think they were mistaken. I am quite certain if she had known anything she must have told it, and, in the next place, the phrase "but there" was not uncommon amongst women in our town, and was supposed to mark the consciousness of a prudently restrained ability to give an explanation of mysterious phenomena in human relationships. For my own part, I am just as much in the dark as my mother. My father, who was a shrewd man, was always puzzled, and could not read the riddle. He used to say that he never thought George could have "made up" to any young woman, and it was quite clear that Miss Leroy did not either then or afterwards display any violent affection for him. I have heard her criticise and patronise him as a "good soul," but incapable, as indeed he was, of all sympathy with her. After marriage she went her way and he his. She got up early, as she was wont to do, and took her Bible into the fields while he was snoring. She would then very likely suffer from a terrible headache during the rest of the day, and lie down for hours, letting the house manage itself as best it could. What made her selection of George more obscure was that she was much admired by many young fellows, some of whom were certainly more akin to her than he was; and I have heard from one or two reports of encouraging words, and even something more than words, which she had vouchsafed to them. A solution is impossible. The affinities, repulsions, reasons in a nature like that of Miss Leroy's are so secret and so subtle, working towards such incalculable and not-to-be-predicted results, that to attempt to make a major and minor premiss and an inevitable conclusion out of them would be useless. One thing was clear, that by marrying George she gained great freedom. If she had married anybody closer to her, she might have jarred with him; there might have been collision and wreck as complete as if they had been entirely opposed; for she was not the kind of person to accommodate herself to others even in the matter of small differences. But George's road through space lay entirely apart from hers, and there was not the slightest chance of interference. She was under the protection of a husband; she could do things that, as an unmarried woman, especially in a foreign land, she could not do, and the compensatory sacrifice to her was small. This is really the only attempt at elucidation I can give. She went regularly all her life to chapel with George, but even when he became deacon, and "supplied" the villages round, she never would join the church as a member. She never agreed with the minister, and he never could make anything out of her. They did not quarrel, but she thought nothing of his sermons, and he was perplexed and uncomfortable in the presence of a nondescript who did not respond to any dogmatic statement of the articles of religion, and who yet could not be put aside as "one of those in the gallery"--that is to say, as one of the ordinary unconverted, for she used to quote hymns with amazing fervour, and she quoted them to him with a freedom and a certain superiority which he might have expected from an aged brother minister, but certainly not from one of his own congregation. He was a preacher of the Gospel, it was true; and it was his duty, a duty on which he insisted, to be "instant in season and out of season" in saying spiritual things to his flock; but then they were things proper, decent, conventional, uttered with gravity at suitable times- -such as were customary amongst all the ministers of the denomination. It was not pleasant to be outbid in his own department, especially by one who was not a communicant, and to be obliged, when he went on a pastoral visit to a house in which Mrs. Butts happened to be, to sit still and hear her, regardless of the minister's presence, conclude a short mystical monologue with Cowper's verse -

> "Exults our rising soul,
>   Disburdened of her load,
> And swells unutterably full
>   Of glory and of God."

   This was NOT pleasant to our minister, nor was it pleasant to the minister's wife. But George Butts held a responsible position in our community, and the minister's wife held also a responsible position, so that she taxed all her ingenuity to let her friends understand at tea-parties what she thought of Mrs. Butts without saying anything which could be the ground of formal remonstrance. Thus did Mrs. Butts live among us, as an Arabian bird with its peculiar habits, cries, and plumage might live in one of our barn-yards with the ordinary barn-door fowls.

   I was never happier when I was a boy than when I was with Mrs. Butts at the mill, which George had inherited. There was a grand freedom in her house. The front door leading into the garden was always open. There was no precise separation between the house and the mill. The business and the dwelling-place were mixed up together, and covered with flour. Mr. Butts was in the habit of walking out of his mill into the living-room every now and then, and never dreamed when one o'clock came that it was necessary for him to change his floury coat before he had his dinner. His cap he also often retained, and in any weather, not extraordinarily cold, he sat in his shirtsleeves. The garden was large and half-wild. A man from the mill, if work was slack, gave a day to it now and then, but it was not trimmed and raked and combed like the other gardens in the town. It was full of gooseberry trees, and I was permitted to eat the gooseberries without stint. The mill-life, too, was inexpressibly attractive--the dark chamber with the great, green, dripping wheel in it, so awfully mysterious as the central life of the whole structure; the machinery connected with the wheel--I knew not how; the hole where the roach lay by the side of the mill-tail in the eddy; the haunts of the water-rats which we used to hunt with Spot, the black and tan terrier, and the still more exciting sport with the ferrets-- all this drew me down the lane perpetually. I liked, and even loved Mrs. Butts, too, for her own sake. Her kindness to me was unlimited, and she was never overcome with the fear of "spoiling me," which seemed the constant dread of most of my hostesses. I never lost my love for her. It grew as I grew, despite my mother's scarcely suppressed hostility to her, and when I heard she was ill, and was likely to die, I went to be with her. She was eighty years old then. I sat by her bedside with her hand in mine. I was there when she passed away, and--but I have no mind and no power to say any more, for all the memories of her affection and of the sunny days by the water come over me and prevent the calmness necessary for a chronicle. She with all her faults and eccentricities will always have in my heart a little chapel with an ever-burning light. She was one of the very very few whom I have ever seen who knew how to love a child.

Mrs. Butts and George had one son who was named Clement. He was exactly my own age, and naturally we were constant companions. We went to the same school. He never distinguished himself at his books, but he was chief among us. He had a versatile talent for almost every accomplishment in which we delighted, but he was not supreme in any one of them. There were better cricketers, better foot-ball players, better hands at setting a night-line, better swimmers than Clem, but he could do something, and do it well, in all these departments. He generally took up a thing with much eagerness for a time, and then let it drop. He was foremost in introducing new games and new fashions, which he permitted to flourish for a time, and then superseded. As he grew up he displayed a taste for drawing and music. He was soon able to copy little paintings of flowers, or even little country scenes, and to play a piece of no very great difficulty with tolerable effect. But as he never was taught by a master, and never practised elementary exercises and studies, he was deficient in accuracy. When the question came what was to be done with him after he left school, his father naturally wished him to go into the mill. Clem, however, set his face steadily against this project, and his mother, who was a believer in his genius, supported him. He actually wanted to go to the University, a thing unheard of in those days amongst our people; but this was not possible, and after dangling about for some time at home, he obtained the post of usher in a school, an occupation which he considered more congenial and intellectual than that of grinding flour. Strange to say, although he knew less than any of his colleagues, he succeed-ed better than any of them. He managed to impress a sense of his own importance upon everybody, including the headmaster. He slid into a position of superiority. above three or four colleagues who would have shamed him at an examination, and who uttered many a curse because they saw themselves surpassed and put in the shade by a stranger, who, they were confident, could hardly construct a hexameter. He never quarrelled with them nor did he grossly patronise them, but he always let them know that he considered himself above them. His reading was desultory; in fact, everything he did was desultory. He was not selfish in the ordinary sense of the word. Rather was he distinguished by a large and liberal open- handedness; but he was liberal also to himself to a remarkable degree, dressing himself expensively, and spending a good deal of money in luxuries. He was specially fond of insisting on his half French origin, made a great deal of his mother, was silent as to his father, and always signed himself C. Leroy Butts, although I don't believe the second Christian name was given him in baptism. Notwithstanding his generosity he was egotistical and hollow at heart. He knew nothing of friendship in the best sense of the word, but had a multitude of acquaintances, whom he invariably sought amongst those who were better off than himself. He was popular with them, for no man knew better than he how to get up an entertainment, or to make a success of an evening party. He had not been at his school for two years before he conceived the notion of setting up for himself. He had not a penny, but he borrowed easily what was wanted from somebody he knew, and in a twelvemonth more he had a dozen pupils. He took care to get the ablest subordinates he could find, and he succeeded in passing a boy for an open scholarship at Oxford, against two competitors prepared by the very man whom he had formerly served. After this he prospered greatly, and would have prospered still more, if his love of show and extravagance had not increased with his income. His talents were sometimes taxed when people who came to place their sons with him supposed ignorantly that his origin and attainments were what might be expected from his position; and poor Chalmers, a Glasgow M.A., who still taught, for 80 pounds a year, the third class in the establishment in which Butts began life, had some bitter stories on that subject. Chalmers was a perfect scholar, but he was not agreeable. He had black finger-nails, and wore dirty collars. Having a lively remembrance of his friend's "general acquaintance" with Latin prosody, Chalmers' opinion of Providence was much modified when he discovered what Providence was doing for Butts. Clem took to the Church when he started for himself. It would have been madness in him to remain a Dissenter. But in private, if it suited his purpose, he could always be airily sceptical, and he had a superficial acquaintance, second-hand, with a multitude of books, many of them of an infidel turn. I once rebuked him for his hypocrisy, and his defence was that religious disputes were indifferent to him, and that at any rate a man associates with gentlemen if he is a churchman. Cultivation and manners he thought to be of more importance than Calvinism. I believe that he partly meant what he said. He went to church because the school would have failed if he had gone to chapel;

but he was sufficiently keen-sighted and clever to be beyond the petty quarrels of the sects, and a song well sung was of much greater moment to him than an essay on paedo- baptism. It was all very well of Chalmers to revile him for his shallowness. He was shallow, and yet he possessed in some mysterious way a talent which I greatly coveted, and which in this world is inestimably precious--the talent of making people give way before him--a capacity of self-impression. Chalmers could never have commanded anybody. He had no power whatever, even when he was right, to put his will against the wills of others, but yielded first this way and then the other. Clem, on the contrary, without any difficulty or any effort, could conquer all opposition, and smilingly force everybody to do his bidding.

Clem had a peculiar theory with regard to his own rights and those of the class to which he considered that he belonged. He always held implicitly and sometimes explicitly that gifted people live under a kind of dispensation of grace; the law existing solely for dull souls. What in a clown is a crime punishable by the laws of the land might in a man of genius be a necessary development, or at any rate an excusable offence. He had nothing to say for the servant-girl who had sinned with the shopman, but if artist or poet were to carry off another man's wife, it might not be wrong.

He believed, and acted upon the belief, that the inferior ought to render perpetual incense to the superior, and that the superior should receive it as a matter of course. When his father was ill he never waited on him or sat up a single night with him. If duty was disagreeable to him Clem paid homage to it afar off, but pleaded exemption. He admitted that waiting on the sick is obligatory on people who are fitted for it, and is very charming. Nothing was more beautiful to him than tender, filial care spending itself for a beloved object. But it was not his vocation. His nerves were more finely ordered than those of mankind generally, and the sight of disease and suffering distressed him too much. Everything was surrendered to him in the houses of his friends. If any inconvenience was to be endured, he was the first person to be protected from it, and he accepted the greatest sacrifices, with a graceful acknowledgment, it is true, but with no repulse. To what better purpose could the best wine be put than in cherishing his imagination. It was simple waste to allow it to be poured out upon the earth, and to give it to a fool was no better. After he succeeded so well in the world, Clem, to a great extent, deserted me, although I was his oldest friend and the friend of his childhood. I heard that he visited a good many rich persons, that he made much of them, and they made much of him. He kept up a kind of acquaintance with me, not by writing to me, but by the very cheap mode of sending me a newspaper now and then with a marked paragraph in it announcing the exploits of his school at a cricket-match, or occasionally with a report of a lecture which he had delivered. He was a decent orator, and from motives of business if from no other, he not unfrequently spoke in public. One or two of these lectures wounded me a good deal. There was one in particular on As You Like It, in which he held up to admiration the fidelity which is so remarkable in Shakespeare, and lamented that in these days it was so rare to find anything of the kind, he thought that we were becoming more indifferent to one another. He maintained, however, that man should be everything to man, and he then enlarged on the duty of really cultivating affection, of its superiority to books, and on the pleasure and profit of self-denial. I do not mean to accuse Clem of downright hypocrisy. I have known many persons come up from the country and go into raptures over a playhouse sun and moon who have never bestowed a glance or a thought on the real sun and moon to be seen from their own doors; and we are all aware it by no means follows because we are moved to our very depths by the spectacle of unrecognised, uncomplaining endurance in a novel, that therefore we can step over the road to waste an hour or a sixpence upon the unrecognised, uncomplaining endurance of the poor lone woman left a widow in the little villa there. I was annoyed with myself because Clem's abandonment of me so much affected me. I wished I could cut the rope and carelessly cast him adrift as he had cast me adrift, but I could not. I never could make out and cannot make out what was the secret of his influence over me; why I was unable to say, "If you do not care for me I do not care for you." I longed sometimes for complete rupture, so that we might know exactly where we were, but it never came. Gradually our intercourse grew thinner and thinner, until at last I heard that he had been spending a fortnight with some semi-aristocratic acquaintance within five miles of me, and during the whole of that time he never came near me. I met him in a railway station soon afterwards, when he came up to me effusive and apparently affectionate. "It was a real grief to me, my dear fellow," he said, "that I could not call on you last month, but the truth was I was so driven: they would make me go here and go there, and I kept putting off my visit to you till it was too late." Fortunately my train was just starting, or I don't know what might have happened. I said not a word; shook hands with him; got into the carriage; he waved his hat to me, and I pretended not to see him, but I did see him, and saw him turn round immediately to some well- dressed officer-like gentleman with whom he walked laughing down the platform. The rest of that day was black to me. I cared for nothing. I passed away from the thought of Clem, and dwelt upon the conviction which had long possessed me that I was INSIGNIFICANT, that there was NOTHING MUCH IN ME, and it was this which destroyed my peace. We may reconcile ourselves to poverty and suffering, but few of us can endure the conviction that there is NOTHING IN US, and that consequently we cannot expect anybody to gravitate towards us with any forceful impulse. It is a bitter experience. And yet there is consolation. The universe is infinite. In the presence of its celestial magnitudes who is there who is really great or small, and what is the difference between you and me, my work and yours? I sought refuge in the idea of GOD, the God of a starry night with its incomprehensible distances; and I was at peace, content to be the meanest worm of all the millions that crawl on the earth.

CHAPTER IV--A NECESSARY DEVELOPMENT

The few friends who have read the first part of my autobiography may perhaps remember that in my younger days I had engaged myself to a girl named Ellen, from whom afterwards I parted. After some two or three years she was left an orphan, and came into the possession of a small property, over which unfortunately she had complete power. She was attractive and well-educated, and I heard long after I had broken with her, and had ceased to have intercourse with Butts, that the two were married. He of course, living so near her, had known her well, and he found her money useful. How they agreed I knew not save by report, but I was told that after the first child was born, the only child they ever had, Butts grew indifferent to her, and that she, to use my friend's expression, "went off," by which I suppose he meant that she faded. There happened in those days to live near Butts a small squire, married, but with no family. He was a lethargic creature, about five-and-thirty years old, farming eight hundred acres of his own land. He did not, however, belong to the farming class. He had been to Harrow, was on the magistrates' bench, and associated with the small aristocracy of the country round. He was like every other squire whom I remember in my native county, and I can remember scores of them. He read no books and tolerated the usual conventional breaches of the moral law, but was an intense worshipper of respectability, and hated a scandal. On one point he differed from his neighbours. He was a Whig and they were all Tories. I have said he read no books, and this, on the whole, is true, but nevertheless he did know something about the history of the early part of the century, and he was rather fond at political gatherings of making some allusion to Mr. Fox. His father had sat in the House of Commons when Fox was there, and had sternly opposed the French war. I don't suppose that anybody not actually IN IT--no Londoner certainly--can understand the rigidity of the bonds which restricted county society when I was young, and for aught I know may restrict it now. There was with us one huge and dark exception to the general uniformity. The earl had broken loose, had ruined his estate, had defied decorum and openly lived with strange women at home and in Paris, but this black background did but set off the otherwise universal adhesion to the Church and to authorised manners, an adhesion tempered and rendered tolerable by port wine. It must not, however, be supposed that human nature was different from the human nature of to-day or a thousand years ago. There were then, even as there were a thousand years ago, and are to-day, small, secret doors, connected with mysterious staircases, by which access was gained to freedom; and men and women, inmates of castles with walls a yard thick, and impenetrable portcullises, sought those doors and descended those stairs night and day. But nobody knew, or if we did know, the silence was profound. The broad-shouldered, yellow- haired Whig squire, had a wife who was the opposite of him. She came from a distant part of the country, and had been educated in France. She was small, with black hair, and yet with blue eyes. She spoke French perfectly, was devoted to music, read French books, and, although she was a constant attendant at church, and gave no opportunity what- ever for the slightest suspicion, the matrons of the circle in which she moved were never quite happy about her. This was due partly to her knowledge of French, and partly to her having no children. Anything more about her I do not know. She was beyond us, and although I have seen her often enough I never spoke to her. Butts, however, managed to become a visitor at the squire's house. Fancy MY go- ing to the squire's! But Butts did, was accepted there, and even dined there with a parson, and two or three half-pay officers. The squire never called on Butts. That was an understood thing, nor did Mrs. Butts accompany her husband. That also was an understood thing. It was strange that Butts could tolerate and even court such a relationship. Most men would scorn with the scorn of a personal insult an invitation to a house from which their wives were expressly excluded. The squire's lady and Clem became great friends. She discovered that his mother was a Frenchwoman, and this was a bond between them. She discovered also that Clem was artistic, that he was devotedly fond of music, that he could draw a little, paint a little, and she believed in the divine right of talent wherever it might be found to assert a claim of equality with those who were better born. The women in the country-side were shy of her; for the men she could not possibly care, and no doubt she must at times have got rather weary of her heavy husband with his one outlook towards the universal in the person of George James Fox, and the Whig policy of 1802. I am under some disadvantage in telling this part of my story, because I was far away from home, and only knew afterwards at second hand what the course of events had been; but I learned them from one who was intimately concerned, and I do not think I can be mistaken on any essential point. I imagine that by this time Mrs. Butts must have become changed into what she was in later years. She had grown older since she and I had parted; she had seen trouble; her child had been born, and although she was not exactly estranged from Clem, for neither he nor she would have admitted any coolness, she had learned that she was nothing specially to him. I have often noticed what an imperceptible touch, what a slight shifting in the balance of opposing forces, will alter the character. I have observed a woman, for example, essentially the same at twenty and thirty--who is there who is not always essentially the same?--and yet, what was a defect at twenty, has become transformed and transfigured into a benignant virtue at thirty; translating the whole nature from the human to the divine. Some slight depression has been wrought here, and some slight lift has been given there, and beauty and order have miraculously emerged from what was chaotic. The same thing may continually be noticed in the hereditary transmission of qualities. The redeeming virtue of the father palpably present in the son becomes his curse, through a faint diminution of the strength of the check which caused that virtue to be the father's salvation. The propensity, too, which is a man's evil genius, and leads him to madness and utter ruin, gives vivid reality to all his words and thoughts, and becomes all his strength, if by divine assistance it can just be subdued and prevented from rising in victorious insurrection. But this is a digression, useful, however, in its way, because it will explain Mrs. Butts when we come a little nearer to her in the future.

For a time Clem's visits to the squire's house always took place when the squire was at home, but an amateur concert was to be arranged in which Clem was to take part together with the squire's lady. Clem consequently was obliged to go to the Hall for the purpose of practising, and so it came to pass that he was there at unusual hours and when the master was afield. These morning and afternoon calls did not cease when the concert was over. Clem's wife did not know anything about them, and, if she noticed his frequent absence, she was met with an excuse. Perhaps the worst, or almost the worst effect of relationships which we do not like to acknowledge, is the secrecy and equivocation which they beget. From the very first moment when the intimacy between the squire's wife and Clem began to be anything more than harmless, he was compelled to shuffle and to become contemptible. At the same time I believe he defended himself against himself with the weapons which were ever ready when self rose against self because of some wrong-doing. He was not as other men. It was absurd to class what he did with what an ordinary person might do, although externally his actions and those of the ordinary person might resemble one another. I cannot trace the steps by which the two sinners drew nearer and nearer together, for the simple reason that this is an autobiography, and not a novel. I do not know what the development was, nor did anybody except the person concerned. Neither do I know what was the mental history of Mrs. Butts during this unhappy period. She seldom talked about it afterwards. I do, however, happen to recollect hearing her once say that her greatest trouble was the cessation, from some unknown cause, of Clem's attempts--they were never many--to interest and amuse her. It is easy to understand how this should be. If a man is guilty of any defection from himself, of anything of which he is ashamed, everything which is better becomes a farce to him. After he has been betrayed by some passion, how can he pretend to the perfect enjoyment of what is pure? The moment he feels any disposition to rise, he is stricken through as if with an arrow, and he drops. Not until weeks, months, and even years have elapsed, does he feel justified in surrendering himself to a noble emotion. I have heard of persons who have been able to ascend easily and instantaneously from the mud to the upper air, and descend as easily; but to me at least they are incomprehensible. Clem, less than most men, suffered permanently, or indeed in any way from remorse, because he was so shielded by his peculiar philosophy; but I can quite believe that when he got into the habit of calling at the Hall at mid-day, his behaviour to his wife changed.

One day in December the squire had gone out with the hounds. Clem, going on from bad to worse, had now reached the point of planning to be at the Hall when the squire was not at home. On that particular afternoon Clem was there. It was about half-past four o'clock, and the master was not expected till six. There had been some music, the lady accompanying, and Clem singing. It was over, and

Clem, sitting down beside her at the piano, and pointing out with his right hand some passage which had troubled him, had placed his left arm on her shoulder, and round her neck, she not resisting. He always swore afterwards that never till then had such a familiarity as this been permitted, and I believe that he did not tell a lie. But what was there in that familiarity? The worst was already there, and it was through a mere accident that it never showed itself. The accident was this. The squire, for some unknown reason, had returned earlier than usual, and dismounting in the stable-yard, had walked round the garden on the turf which came close to the windows of the ground floor. Passing the drawing-room window, and looking in by the edge of the drawn-down blind, he saw his wife and Clem just at the moment described. He slipped round to the door, took off his boots so that he might not be heard, and as there was a large screen inside the room he was able to enter it unobserved. Clem caught sight of him just as he emerged from behind the screen, and started up instantly in great confusion, the lady, with greater presence of mind, remaining perfectly still. Without a word the squire strode up to Clem, struck out at him, caught him just over the temple, and felled him instantaneously. He lay for some time senseless, and what passed between husband and wife I cannot say. After about ten minutes, perhaps, Clem came to himself; there was nobody to be seen; and he managed to get up and crawl home. He told his wife he had met with an accident; that he would go to bed, and that she should know all about it when he was better. His forehead was dressed, and to bed he went. That night Mrs. Butts had a letter. It ran as follows:-

"MADAM,--It may at first sight seem a harsh thing for me to write and tell you what I have to say, but I can assure you I do not mean to be anything but kind to you, and I think it will be better, for reasons which I will afterwards explain, that I should communicate with you rather than with your husband. For some time past I have suspected that he was too fond of my wife, and last night I caught him with his arms round her neck. In a moment of not unjustifiable anger I knocked him down. I have not the honour of knowing you personally, but from what I have heard of you I am sure that he has not the slightest reason for playing with other women. A man who will do what he has done will be very likely to conceal from you the true cause of his disaster, and if you know the cause you may perhaps be able to re-claim him. If he has any sense of honour left in him, and of what is due to you, he will seek your pardon for his baseness, and you will have a hold on him afterwards which you would not have if you were in ignorance of what has happened. For him I do not care a straw, but for you I feel deeply, and I believe that my frankness with you, although it may cause you much suffering now, will save you more hereafter. I have only one condition to make. Mr. Butts must leave this place, and never let me see his face again. He has ruined my peace. Nothing will be published through me, for, as far as I can prevent it, I will have no public exposure. If Mr. Butts were to remain here it would be dangerous for us to meet, and probably everything, by some chance, would become common property.--Believe me to be, Madam, with many assurances of respect, truly yours,--."

I cannot distinguish the precise proportion of cruelty in this letter. Did the writer designedly torture Butts by telling his wife, or did he really think that she would in the end be happier because Butts would not have a secret reserved from her,--a temptation to lying--and because with this secret in her possession, he might perhaps be restrained in future? Nobody knows. All we know is that there are very few human actions of which it can be said that this or that taken by itself produced them. With our inborn tendency to abstract, to separate mentally the concrete into factors which do not exist separately, we are always disposed to assign causes which are too simple, and which, in fact, have no being in rerum natura. Nothing in nature is propelled or impeded by one force acting alone. There is no such thing, save in the brain of the mathematician. I see no reason why even motives diametrically opposite should not unite in one resulting deed, and think it very probable that the squire was both cruel and merciful to the same person in the letter; influenced by exactly conflicting passions, whose conflict ended SO.

As to the squire and his wife, they lived together just as before. I do not think, that, excepting the four persons concerned, anybody ever heard a syllable about the affair, save myself a long while afterwards. Clem, however, packed up and left the town, after selling his business. He had a reputation for restlessness; and his departure, although it was sudden, was no surprise. He betook himself to Australia, his wife going with him. I heard that they had gone, and heard also that he was tired of school-keeping in England, and had determined to try his fortune in another part of the world. Our friendship had dwindled to nothing, and I thought no more about him. Mrs. Butts never uttered one word of reproach to her husband. I cannot say that she loved him as she could have loved, but she had accepted him, and she said to herself that as perhaps it was through her lack of sympathy with him that he had strayed, it was her duty more and more to draw him to herself. She had a divine disposition, not infrequent amongst women, to seek in herself the reason for any wrong which was done to her. That almost instinctive tendency in men, to excuse, to transfer blame to others, to be angry with somebody else when they suffer from the consequences of their own misdeeds, in her did not exist.

During almost the whole of her married life, before this affair between the squire and Clem, Mrs. Butts had had much trouble, although her trouble was, perhaps, rather the absence of joy than the presence of any poignant grief. She was much by herself. She had never been a great reader, but in her frequent solitude she was forced to do something in order to obtain relief, and she naturally turned to the Bible. It would be foolish to say that the Bible alone was to be credited with the support she received. It may only have been the occasion for a revelation of the strength that was in her. Reading, however, under such circumstances, is likely to be peculiarly profitable. It is never so profitable as when it is undertaken in order that a positive need may be satisfied or an inquiry answered. She discovered in the Bible much that persons to whom it is a mere literature would never find. The water of life was not merely admirable to the eye; she drank it, and knew what a property it possessed for quenching thirst. No doubt the thought of a heaven hereafter was especially consolatory. She was able to endure, and even to be happy because the vision of lengthening sorrow was bounded by a better world beyond. "A very poor, barbarous gospel," thinks the philosopher who rests on his Marcus Antoninus and Epictetus. I do not mean to say, that in the shape in which she believed this doctrine, it was not poor and barbarous, but yet we all of us, whatever our creed may be, must lay hold at times for salvation upon something like it. Those who have been plunged up to the very lips in affliction know its necessity. To such as these it is idle work for the prosperous and the comfortable to preach satisfaction with the life that now is. There are seasons when it is our sole resource to recollect that in a few short years we shall be at rest. While upon this subject I may say, too, that some injustice has been done to the Christian creed of immortality as an influence in determining men's conduct. Paul preached the imminent advent of Christ and besought his disciples, therefore, to watch, and we ask ourselves what is the moral value to us of such an admonition. But surely if we are to have any reasons for being virtuous, this is as good as any other. It is just as respectable to believe that we ought to abstain from iniquity because Christ is at hand, and we expect to meet Him, as to abstain from it because by our abstention we shall be healthier or more prosperous. Paul had a dream--an absurd dream let us call it--of an immediate millennium, and of the return of his Master surrounded with divine splendour, judging mankind and adjusting the balance between good and evil. It was a baseless dream, and the enlightened may call it ridiculous. It is anything but that, it is the very opposite of that. Putting aside its temporary mode of expression, it is the hope and the prophecy of all noble hearts, a sign of their inability to concur in the present condition of things.

Going back to Clem's wife; she laid hold, as I have said, upon heaven. The thought wrought in her something more than forgetfulness of pain or the expectation of counterpoising bliss. We can understand what this something was, for although we know no such heaven as hers, a new temper is imparted to us, a new spirit breathed into us; I was about to say a new hope bestowed upon us, when we consider that we live surrounded by the soundless depths in which the stars repose. Such a consideration has a direct practical effect upon us, and so had the future upon the mind of Mrs. Butts. "Why dost thou judge thy brother," says Paul, "for we shall all stand before the judgment-seat of God." Paul does not mean that God will punish him and that we may rest satisfied that our enemy will be turned into hell fire. Rather does he mean, what we, too, feel, that, reflecting on the great idea of God, and upon all that it involves, our animosities are softened, and our heat against our brother is cooled.

One or two reflections may perhaps be permitted here on this passage in Mrs. Butts' history.

The fidelity of Clem's wife to him, if not entirely due to the New Testament, was in a great measure traceable to it. She had learned from the Epistle to the Corinthians that charity beareth all things, believeth all things, hopeth all things, endureth all things; and she interpreted this to mean, not merely charity to those whom she loved by nature, but charity to those with whom she was not in sympathy, and who even wronged her. Christianity no doubt does teach such a charity as this, a love which is to be: independent of mere personal likes and dislikes, a love of the human in man. The natural man, the man of this century, uncontrolled by Christianity, considers himself a model of what is virtuous and heroic if he really loves his friends, and he permits all kinds of savage antipathies to those of his fellow creatures with whom he is not in harmony. Jesus on the other hand asks with His usual perfect simplicity, "If ye love them which love you, what reward have ye? Do not even the publicans the same?" It would be a great step in advance for most of us to love anybody, and the publicans of the time of Jesus must have been a much more Christian set than most Christians of the present day; but that we should love those who do not love us is a height never scaled now, except by a few of the elect in whom Christ still survives. In the gospel of Luke, also, Mrs. Butts read that she was to hope for nothing again from her love, and that she was to be merciful, as her Father in heaven is merciful. That is really the expression of the IDEA in morality, and incalculable is the blessing that our great religious teacher should have been bold enough to teach the idea, and not any limitation of it. He always taught it, the inward born, the heavenly law towards which everything strives. He always trusted it; He did not deal in exceptions; He relied on it to the uttermost, never despairing. This has always seemed to me to be the real meaning of the word faith. It is permanent confidence in the idea, a confidence never to be broken down by apparent failure, or by examples by which ordinary people prove that qualification is necessary. It was precisely because Jesus taught the idea, and nothing below it, that He had such authority over a soul like my friend's, and the effect produced by Him could not have been produced by anybody nearer to ordinary humanity.

It must be admitted, too, that the Calvinism of those days had a powerful influence in enabling men and women to endure, although I object to giving the name of Calvin to a philosophy which is a necessity in all ages. "Are not two sparrows sold for a farthing? and one of them shall not fall on the ground without your Father." This is the last word which can be said. Nothing can go beyond it, and at times it is the only ground which we feel does not shake under our feet. All life is summed up, and due account is taken of it, according to its degree. Mrs. Butts' Calvinism, however, hardly took the usual dogmatic form. She was too simple to penetrate the depths of metaphysical theology, and she never would have dared to set down any of her fellow creatures as irrevocably lost. She adapted the Calvinistic creed to something which suited her. For example, she fully understood what

St. Paul means when he tells the Thessalonians that BECAUSE they were called, THEREFORE they were to stand fast. She thought with Paul that being called; having a duty plainly laid upon her; being bidden as if by a general to do something, she OUGHT to stand fast; and she stood fast, supported against all pressure by the consciousness of fulfilling the special orders of One who was her superior. There is no doubt that this dogma of a personal calling is a great consolation, and it is a great truth. Looking at the masses of humanity, driven this way and that way, the Christian teaching is apt to be forgotten that for each individual soul there is a vocation as real as if that soul were alone upon the planet. Yet it is a fact. We are blinded to it and can hardly believe it, because of the impotency of our little intellects to conceive a destiny which shall take care of every atom of life on the globe: we are compelled to think that in such vast crowds of people as we behold, individuals must elude the eye of the Maker, and be swept into forgetfulness. But the truth of truths is that the mind of the universe is not our mind, or at any rate controlled by our limitations.

This has been a long digression which I did not intend; but I could not help it. I was anxious to show how Mrs. Butts met her trouble through her religion. The apostle says that "they drank of that spiritual Rock which followed them, and that Rock was Christ." That was true of her. The way through the desert was not annihilated; the path remained stony and sore to the feet, but it was accompanied to the end by a sweet stream to which she could turn aside, and from which she could obtain refreshment and strength.

Just about the time that we began our meetings near Drury Lane, I heard that Clem was dead; that he had died abroad. I knew nothing more; I thought about him and his wife perhaps for a day, but I had parted from both long ago, and I went on with my work.

CHAPTER V--WHAT IT ALL CAME TO

For two years or thereabouts, M'Kay and myself continued our labours in the Drury Lane neighbourhood. There is a proverb that it is the first step which is the most difficult in the achievement of any object, and the proverb has been altered by ascribing the main part of the difficulty to the last step. Neither the first nor the last has been the difficult step with me, but rather what lies between. The first is usually helped by the excitement and the promise of new beginnings, and the last by the prospect of triumph; but the intermediate path is unassisted by enthusiasm, and it is here we are so likely to faint. M'Kay nevertheless persevered, supporting me, who otherwise might have been tempted to despair, and at the end of the two years we were still at our posts. We had, however, learned something. We had learned that we could not make the slightest impression on Drury Lane proper. Now and then an idler, or sometimes a dozen, lounged in, but what was said was strange to them; they were out of their own world as completely as if they were in another planet, and all our efforts to reach them by simplicity of statement and by talking about things which we supposed would interest them utterly failed. I did not know, till I came in actual contact with them, how far away the classes which lie at the bottom of great cities are from those above them; how completely they are inaccessible to motives which act upon ordinary human beings, and how deeply they are sunk beyond ray of sun or stars, immersed in the selfishness naturally begotten of their incessant struggle for existence and the incessant warfare with society. It was an awful thought to me, ever present on those Sundays, and haunting me at other times, that men, women, and children were living in such brutish degradation, and that as they died others would take their place. Our civilisation seemed nothing but a thin film or crust lying over a volcanic pit, and I often wondered whether some day the pit would not break up through it and destroy us all. Great towns are answerable for the creation and maintenance of the masses of dark, impenetrable, subterranean blackguardism, with which we became acquainted. The filthy gloom of the sky, the dirt of the street, the absence of fresh air, the herding of the poor into huge districts which cannot be opened up by those who would do good, are tremendous agencies of corruption which are active at such a rate that it is appalling to reflect what our future will be if the accumulation of population be not checked. To stand face to face with the insoluble is not pleasant. A man will do anything rather than confess it is beyond him. He will create pleasant fictions, and fancy a possible escape here and there, but this problem of Drury Lane was round and hard like a ball of adamant. The only thing I could do was faintly, and I was about to say stupidly, hope--for I had no rational, tangible grounds for hoping--that some force of which we are not now aware might some day develop itself which will be able to resist and remove the pressure which sweeps and crushes into a hell, sealed from the upper air, millions of human souls every year in one quarter of the globe alone.

M'Kay's dreams therefore were not realised, and yet it would be a mistake to say that they ended in nothing. It often happens that a grand attempt, although it may fail--miserably fail--is fruitful in the end and leaves a result, not the hoped for result it is true, but one which would never have been attained without it. A youth strives after the impossible, and he is apt to break his heart because he has never even touched it, but nevertheless his whole life is the sweeter for the striving; and the archer who aims at a mark a hundred yards away will send his arrow further than he who sets his bow and his arm for fifty yards. So it was with M'Kay. He did not convert Drury Lane, but he saved two or three. One man whom we came to know was a labourer in Somerset House, a kind of coal porter employed in carrying coals into the offices there from the cellars below, and in other menial duties. He had about fifteen or sixteen shillings a week, and as the coals must necessarily be in the different rooms before ten o'clock in the morning, he began work early, and was obliged to live within an easy distance of the Strand. This man had originally been a small tradesman in a country town. He was honest, but he never could or never would push his trade in any way. He was fond of all kinds of little mechanical contrivings, disliked his shop, and ought to have been a carpenter or cabinet-maker--not as a master but as a journeyman, for he had no ability whatever to control men or direct large operations. He was married, and a sense of duty to his wife--he fortunately had no children--induced him to stand or sit behind his counter with regularity, but people would not come to buy of him, because he never seemed to consider their buying as any favour conferred on him; and thus he became gradually displaced by his more energetic or more obsequious rivals. In the end he was obliged to put up his shutters. Unhappily for him, he had never been a very ardent attendant at any of the places of religious worship in the town, and he had therefore no organisation to help him. Not being master of any craft, he was in a pitiable plight, and was slowly sinking, when he applied to the solicitor of the political party for which he had always voted to assist him. The solicitor applied to the member, and the member, much regretting the difficulty of obtaining places for grown-up men, and explaining the pressure upon the Treasury, wrote to say that the only post at his disposal was that of labourer. He would have liked to offer a messengership, but the Treasury had hundreds of applications from great people who wished to dispose of favourite footmen whose services they no longer required. Our friend Taylor had by this time been brought very low, or he would have held out for something better, but there was nothing to be done. He was starving, and he therefore accepted; came to London; got a room, one room only, near Clare Market, and began his new duties. He was able to pick up a shilling or two more weekly by going on errands for the clerks during his slack time in the day, so that altogether on the average he made up about eighteen shillings. Wandering about the Clare Market region on Sunday he found us out, came in, and remained constant. Naturally, as we had so few adherents, we gradually knew these few very intimately, and Taylor would often spend a holiday or part of the Sunday with us. He was not eminent for anything in particular, and an educated man, selecting as his friends those only who stand for something, would not have taken the slightest notice of him. He had read nothing particular, and thought nothing particular--he was indeed one of the masses--but in this respect different, that he had not the tendency to association, aggregation, or clanship which belong to the masses generally. He was different, of course, in all his ways from his neighbours born and bred to Clare Market and its alleys. Although commonplace, he had demands made upon him for an endurance by no means commonplace, and he had sorrows which were as exquisite as those of his betters. He did not much resent his poverty. To that I think he would have submitted, and in fact he did submit to it cheerfully. What rankled in him was the brutal disregard of him at the office. He was a servant of servants. The messengers, who themselves were exposed to all the petty tyrannies of the clerks, and dared not reply, were Taylor's masters, and sought a compensation for their own serfdom by making his ten times worse. The head messenger, who had been a butler, swore at him, and if Taylor had "answered" he would have been reported. He had never been a person of much importance, but at least he had been independent, and it was a new experience for him to feel that he was a thing fit for nothing but to be cuffed and cursed. Upon this point he used to get eloquent--as eloquent as he could be, for he had small power of expression, and he would describe to me the despair which came over him down in those dark vaults at the prospect of life continuing after this fashion, and with not the minutest gleam of light even at the very end. Nobody ever cared to know the most ordinary facts about him. Nobody inquired whether he was married or single; nobody troubled himself when he was ill. If he was away, his pay was stopped; and when he returned to work nobody asked if he was better. Who can wonder that at first, when he was an utter stranger in a strange land, he was overcome by the situation, and that the world was to him a dungeon worse than that of Chillon? Who can wonder that he was becoming reckless? A little more of such a life would have transformed him into a brute. He had not the ability to become revolutionary, or it would have made him a conspirator. Suffering of any kind is hard to bear, but the suffering which especially damages character is that which is caused by the neglect or oppression of man. At any rate it was so in Taylor's case. I believe that he would have been patient under any inevitable ordinance of nature, but he could not lie still under contempt, the knowledge that to those about him he was of less consequence than the mud under their feet. He was timid and, after his failure as a shopkeeper, and the near approach to the workhouse, he dreaded above everything being again cast adrift. Strange conflict arose in him, for the insults to which he was exposed drove him almost to madness; and yet the dread of dismissal in a moment checked him when he was about to "fire up," as he called it, and reduced him to a silence which was torture. Once he was ordered to bring some coals for the messenger's lobby. The man who gave him the order, finding that he was a long time bringing them, went to the top of the stairs, and bawled after him with an oath to make haste. The reason of the delay was that Taylor had two loads to bring up--one for somebody else. When he got to the top of the steps, the messenger with another oath took the coals, and saying that he "would teach him to skulk there again," kicked the other coal-scuttle down to the bottom. Taylor himself told me this; and yet, although he would have rejoiced if the man had dropped down dead, and would willingly have shot him, he was dumb. The check operated in an instant. He saw himself without a penny, and in the streets. He went down into the cellar, and raged and wept for an hour. Had he been a workman, he would probably have throttled his enemy, or tried to do it, or what is more likely, his enemy would not have dared to treat him in such fashion, but he was powerless, and once losing his situation he would have sunk down into the gutter, whence he would have been swept by the parish into the indiscriminate heap of London pauperism, and carted away to the Union, a conclusion which was worse to him than being hung.

Another of our friends was a waiter in one of the public-houses and chop-houses combined, of which there are so many in the Strand. He lived in a wretched alley which ran from St. Clement's Church to Boswell Court--I have forgotten its name--a dark crowded passage. He was a man of about sixty--invariably called John, without the addition of any surname. I knew him long before we opened our room, for I was in the habit of frequently visiting the chop-house in which he served. His hours were incredible. He began at nine o'clock in the morning with sweeping the dining-room, cleaning the tables and the gas globes, and at twelve business commenced with early luncheons. Not till three-quarters of an hour after midnight could he leave, for the house was much used by persons who supped there after the theatres. During almost the whole of this time he was on his legs, and very often he was unable to find two minutes in the day in which to get his dinner. Sundays, however, were free. John was not a head waiter, but merely a subordinate, and I never knew why at his time of life he had not risen to a better position. He used to say that "things had been against him," and I had no right to seek for further explanations. He was married, and had had three children, of whom one only was living--a boy of ten years old, whom he hoped to get into the public-house as a potboy for a beginning. Like Taylor, the world had well-nigh overpowered John entirely-- crushed him out of all shape, so that what he was originally, or might have been, it was almost impossible to tell. There was no particular character left in him. He may once have been this or that, but every angle now was knocked off, as it is knocked off from the rounded pebbles which for ages have been dragged up and down the beach by the waves. For a lifetime he had been exposed to all sorts of whims and caprices, generally speaking of the most unreasonable kind, and he had become so trained to take everything without remonstrance or murmuring that every cross in his life came to him as a chop alleged by an irritated customer to be raw or done to a cinder. Poor wretch! he had one trouble, however, which he could not accept with such equanimity, or rather with such indifference. His wife was a drunkard. This was an awful trial to him. The worst consequence was that his boy knew that his mother got drunk. The neighbours kindly enough volunteered to look after the little man when he was not at school, and they waylaid him and gave him dinner when his mother was intoxicated; but frequently he was the first when he returned to find out that there was nothing for him to eat, and many a time he got up at night as late as twelve o'clock, crawled downstairs, and went off to his father to tell him that "she was very bad, and he could not go to sleep." The father, then, had to keep his son in the Strand till it was time to close, take him back, and manage in the best way he could. Over and over again was he obliged to sit by this wretched woman's bedside till breakfast time, and then had to go to work as usual. Let anybody who has seen a case of this kind say whether the State ought not to provide for the relief of such men as John, and whether he ought not to have been able to send his wife away to some institution where she might have been tended and restrained from destroying, not merely herself, but her husband and her child. John hardly bore up under this sorrow. A man may endure much, provided he knows that he will be well supported when his day's toil is over; but if the help for which he looks fails, he falls. Oh those weary days in that dark back dining-room, from which not a square inch of sky was visible! weary days haunted by a fear that while he was there unknown mischief was being done! weary days, whose close nevertheless he dreaded! Beaten down, baffled, disappointed, if we are in tolerable health we can contrive to live on some almost impossible chance, some most distant flicker of hope. It is astonishing how minute a crack in the heavy uniform cloud will relieve us; but when with all our searching we can see nothing, then at last we sink. Such was John's case when I first came to know him. He attracted me rather, and bit by bit he confided his story to me. He found out that I might be trusted, and that I could sympathise, and he told me what he had never told to anybody before. I was curious to discover whether religion had done anything for him, and I put the question to him in an indirect way. His answer was that "some on 'em say there's a better world where everything will be put right, but somehow it seemed too good to be true." That was his reason for disbelief, and heaven had not the slightest effect on him. He found out the room, and was one of our most constant friends.

Another friend was of a totally different type. His name was Cardinal. He was a Yorkshireman, broad-shouldered, ruddy in the face, short-necked, inclined apparently to apoplexy, and certainly to passion. He was a commercial traveller in the cloth trade, and as he had the southern counties for his district, London was his home when he was not upon his journeys. His wife was a curious contrast to him. She was dark-haired, pinched-up, thin-lipped, and always seemed as if she suffered from some chronic pain or gnawing--not sufficient to make her ill, but sufficient to make her miserable. They had no children. Cardinal in early life had been a member of an orthodox Dissenting congregation, but he had fallen away. He had nobody to guide him, and the position into which he fell was peculiar. He never busied himself about religion or philosophy; indeed he had had no training which would have led him to take an interest in abstract questions, but he read all kinds of romances and poetry without any order and upon no system. He had no discriminating faculty, and mixed up together the most heterogeneous mass of trumpery novels, French translations, and the best English authors, provided only they were unworldly or sentimental. Neither did he know how far to take what he read and use it in his daily life. He often selected some fantastical motive which he had found set forth as operative in one of his heroes, and he brought it into his business, much to the astonishment of his masters and customers. For this reason he was not stable. He changed employers two or three times; and, so far as I could make out, his ground of objection to each of the firms whom he left might have been a ground of dislike in a girl to a suitor, but certainly nothing more. During the intervals of his engagements, unless he was pressed for money, he did nothing--not from laziness, but because he had got a notion in his head that his mind wanted rest and reinvigoration. His habit then was to consume the whole day--day after day--in reading or in walking out by himself. It may easily be supposed that with a temperament like his, and with nobody near him to take him by the hand, he made great mistakes. His wife and he cared nothing for one another, but she was jealous to the last degree. I never saw such jealousy. It was strange that, although she almost hated him, she watched him with feline sharpness and patience, and would even have killed any woman whom she knew had won his affection. He, on the other hand, openly avowed that marriage without love was nothing, and flaunted without the least modification the most ideal theories as to the relation between man and woman. Not that he ever went actually wrong. His boyish education, his natural purity, and a fear never wholly suppressed, restrained him. He exasperated people by his impracticability, and it must be acknowledged that it is very irritating in a difficult complexity demanding the gravest consideration--the balancing of this against that--to hear a man suddenly propose some naked principle with which everybody is acquainted, and decide by it solely. I came to know him through M'Kay, who had known him for years; but M'Kay at last broke out against him, and called him a stupid fool when he threw up a handsome salary and refused to serve any longer under a house which had always treated him well, because they, moving with the times, had determined to offer their customers a cheaper description of goods, which Cardinal thought was dishonest. M'Kay said, and said truly, that many poor persons would buy these goods who could buy nothing else, and that Cardinal, before yielding to such scruples, ought to satisfy himself that, by yielding, he would not become a burden upon others less fanciful. This was just what happened. Cardinal could get no work again for a long time, and had to borrow money. I was sorry; but for my part, this and other eccentricities did not disturb my confidence in him. He was an honest, affectionate soul, and his peculiarities were a necessary result of the total chaos of a time without any moral guidance. With no church, no philosophy, no religion, the wonder is that anybody on whom use and wont relax their hold should ever do anything more than blindly rove hither and thither, arriving at nothing. Cardinal was adrift, like thousands and hundreds of thousands of others, and amidst the storm and pitchy darkness of the night, thousands and hundreds of thousands of voices offer us pilotage. It spoke well for him that he did nothing worse than take a few useless phantoms on board which did him no harm, and that he held fast to his own instinct for truth and goodness. I never let myself be annoyed by what he produced to me from his books. All that I discarded. Underneath all that was a solid worth which I loved, and which was mostly not vocal.

What was vocal in him was, I am bound to say, not of much value.

About the time when our room opened, Mrs. Cardinal had become almost insupportable to her husband. Poor woman; I always pitied her; she was alone sometimes for a fortnight at a stretch; she read nothing; there was no child to occupy her thoughts; she knew that her husband lived in a world into which she never entered, and she had nothing to do but to brood over imaginary infidelities. She was literally possessed, and who shall be hard upon her? Nobody cared for her; everybody with whom her husband associated disliked her, and she knew perfectly well they never asked her to their houses except for his sake. Cardinal vowed at last he would endure her no longer, and that they must separate. He was induced one Sunday morning, when his resolution was strong within him, and he was just about to give effect to it, to come with us. The quiet seemed to soothe him, and he went home with me afterwards. He was not slow to disclose to me his miserable condition, and his resolve to change it. I do not know now what I said, but it appeared to me that he ought not to change it, and that change would be for him most perilous. I thought that with a little care life might become at least bearable with his wife; that by treating her not so much as if she were criminal, but as if she were diseased, hatred might pass into pity, and pity into merciful tenderness to her, and that they might dwell together upon terms not harder than those upon which many persons who have made mistakes in youth agree to remain with each other; terms which, after much consideration, they adjudge it better to accept than to break loose, and bring upon themselves and those connected with them all that open rupture involves. The difficulty was to get Cardinal to give up his theory of what two abstract human beings should do between whom no love exists. It seemed to him something like atheism to forsake his clearly-discerned, simple rule for a course which was dictated by no easily-grasped higher law, and it was very difficult to persuade him that there is anything of equal authority in a law less rigid in its outline. However, he went home. I called on him some time afterwards, and saw that a peace, or at any rate a truce, was proclaimed, which lasted up to the day of his death. M'Kay and I agreed to make as much of Mrs. Cardinal as we could, and yielding to urgent invitation, she came to the room. This wonderfully helped to heal her. She began to feel that she was not overlooked, put on one side, or despised, and the bonds which bound her constricted lips into bitterness were loosened.

Another friend, and the last whom I shall name, was a young man named Clark. He was lame, and had been so from childhood. His father was a tradesman, working hard from early morning till late at night, and burdened with a number of children. The boy Richard, shut out from the companionship of his fellows, had a great love of books. When he left school his father did not know what to do with him--in fact there was only one occupation open to him, and that was clerical work of one kind or another. At last he got a place in a house in Fleet Street, which did a large business in those days in sending newspapers into the country. His whole occupation all day long was to write addresses, and for this he received twenty-five shillings a week, his hours being from nine o'clock till seven. The office in which he sat was crowded, and in order to squeeze the staff into the smallest space, rent being dear, a gallery had been run round the wall about four feet from the ceiling. This was provided with desks and gas lamps, and up there Clark sat, artificial light being necessary four days out of five. He came straight from the town in which his father lived to Fleet Street, and once settled in it there seemed no chance of change for the better. He knew what his father's struggles were; he could not go back to him, and he had not the energy to attempt to lift himself. It is very doubtful too whether he could have succeeded in achieving any improvement, whatever his energy might have been. He had got lodgings in Newcastle Street, and to these he returned in the evening, remaining there alone with his little library, and seldom moving out of doors. He was unhealthy constitutionally, and his habits contributed to make him more so. Everything which he saw which was good seemed only to sharpen the contrast between himself and his lot, and his reading was a curse to him rather than a blessing. I sometimes wished that he had never inherited any love whatever for what is usually considered to be the Best, and that he had been endowed with an organisation coarse and commonplace, like that of his colleagues. If he went into company which suited him, or read anything which interested him, it seemed as if the ten hours of the gallery in Fleet Street had been made thereby only the more insupportable, and his habitual mood was one of despondency, so that his fellow clerks who knew his tastes not unnaturally asked what was the use of them if they only made him wretched; and they were more than ever convinced that in their amusements lay true happiness. Habit, which is the saviour of most of us, the opiate which dulls the otherwise unbearable miseries of life, only served to make Clark more sensitive. The monotony of that perpetual address-copying was terrible. He has told me with a kind of shame what an effect it had upon him--that sometimes for days he would feed upon the prospect of the most childish trifle because it would break in some slight degree the uniformity of his toil. For example, he would sometimes change from quill to steel pens and back again, and he found himself actually looking forward with a kind of joy--merely because of the variation--to the day on which he had fixed to go back to the quill after using steel. He would determine, two or three days beforehand, to get up earlier, and to walk to Fleet Street by way of Great Queen Street and Lincoln's Inn Fields, and upon this he would subsist till the day came. He could make no longer excursions because of his lameness. All this may sound very much like simple silliness to most people, but those who have not been bound to a wheel do not know what thoughts come into the head of the strongest man who is extended on it. Clark sat side by side in his gallery with other young men of rather a degraded type, and the confinement bred in them a filthy grossness with which they tormented him. They excited in him loathsome images, from which he could not free himself either by day or night. He was peculiarly weak in his inability to cast off impressions, or to get rid of mental pictures when once formed, and his distress at being haunted by these hateful, disgusting thoughts was pitiable. They were in fact almost more than thoughts, they were transportations out of himself--real visions. It would have been his salvation if he could have been a carpenter or a bricklayer, in country air, but this could not be.

Clark had no power to think connectedly to a conclusion. When an idea came into his head, he dwelt upon it incessantly, and no correction of the false path upon which it set him was possible, because he avoided society. Work over, he was so sick of people that he went back to himself. So it came to pass that when brought into company, what he believed and cherished was frequently found to be open to obvious objection, and was often nothing better than nonsense which was rudely, and as he himself was forced to admit, justly overthrown. He ought to have been surrounded with intelligent friends, who would have enabled him to see continually the other side, and who would have prevented his long and useless wanderings. Like many other persons, too, whom I have known--just in proportion to his lack of penetrative power was his tendency to occupy himself with difficult questions.

By a cruel destiny he was impelled to dabble in matters for which he was totally unfitted. He never could go beyond his author a single step, and he lost himself in endless mazes. If he could but have been persuaded to content himself with sweet presentations of wholesome happy existence, with stories and with history, how much better it would have been for him! He had had no proper training whatever for anything more, he was ignorant of the exact meaning of the proper terminology of science, and an unlucky day it was for him when he picked up on a bookstall some very early translation of some German book on philosophy. One reason, as may be conjectured, for his mistakes was his education in dissenting Calvinism, a religion which is entirely metaphysical, and encourages, unhappily, in everybody a taste for tremendous problems. So long as Calvinism is unshaken, the mischief is often not obvious, because a ready solution taken on trust is provided; but when doubts arise, the evil results become apparent, and the poor helpless victim, totally at a loss, is torn first in this direction and then in the other, and cannot let these questions alone. He has been taught to believe they are connected with salvation, and he is compelled still to busy himself with them, rather than with simple external piety.

CHAPTER VI--DRURY LANE THEOLOGY

Such were some of our disciples. I do not think that church or chapel would have done them much good. Preachers are like unskilled doctors with the same pill and draught for every complaint. They do not know where the fatal spot lies on lung or heart or nerve which robs us of life. If any of these persons just described had gone to church or chapel they would have heard discourses on the usual set topics, none of which would have concerned them. Their trouble was not the forgiveness of sins, the fallacies of Arianism, the personality of the Holy Ghost, or the doctrine of the Eucharist. They all WANTED something distinctly. They had great gaping needs which they longed to satisfy, intensely practical and special. Some of these necessities no words could in any way meet. It was obvious, for instance, that Clark must at once be taken away from his gallery and his copying if he was to live--at least in sanity. He had fortunately learned shorthand, and M'Kay got him employment on a newspaper. His knowledge of his art was by no means perfect at first, but he was sent to attend meetings where verbatim reports were not necessary, and he quickly advanced. Taylor, too, we tried to remove, and we succeeded in attaching him to a large club as an out- of-doors porter. The poor man was now at least in the open air, and freed from insolent tyranny. This, however, was help such as anybody might have given. The question of most importance is, What gospel had we to give? Why, in short, did we meet on the Sunday? What was our justification? In the first place, there was the simple quietude. The retreat from the streets and from miserable cares into a place where there was peace and room for reflection was something. It is all very well for cultivated persons with libraries to scoff at religious services. To the poor the cathedral or the church might be an immense benefit, if only for the reason that they present a barrier to worldly noise, and are a distinct invitation by architecture and symbolic decoration to meditation on something beyond the business which presses on them during the week. Poor people frequently cannot read for want of a place in which to read. Moreover, they require to be provoked by a stronger stimulus than that of a book. They willingly hear a man talk if he has anything to say, when they would not care to look at what he said if it were printed. But to come more closely to the point. Our main object was to create in our hearers contentment with their lot; and even some joy in it. That was our religion; that was the central thought of all we said and did, giving shape and tendency to everything. We admitted nothing which did not help us in that direction, and everything which did help us. Our attempts, to any one who had not the key, may have seemed vague and desultory. We might by a stranger have been accused of feeble wandering, of idle dabbling, now in this subject and now in that, but after a while he would have found that though we were weak creatures, with no pretence to special knowledge in any subject, we at least knew what we meant, and tried to accomplish it. For my own part, I was happy when I had struck that path. I felt as if somehow, after many errors, I had once more gained a road, a religion in fact, and one which essentially was not new but old, the religion of the Reconciliation, the reconciliation of man with God; differing from the current creed in so far as I did not lay stress upon sin as the cause of estrangement, but yet agreeing with it in making it my duty of duties to suppress revolt, and to submit calmly and sometimes cheerfully to the Creator. This surely, under a thousand disguises, has been the meaning of all the forms of worship which we have seen in the world. Pain and death are nothing new, and men have been driven into perplexed scepticism, and even insurrection by them, ever since men came into being. Always, however, have the majority, the vast majority of the race, felt instinctively that in this scepticism and insurrection they could not abide, and they have struggled more or less blindly after explanation; determined not to desist till they had found it, and reaching a result embodied in a multitude of shapes irrational and absurd to the superficial scoffer, but of profound interest to the thoughtful. I may observe, in passing, that this is a reason why all great religions should be treated with respect, and in a certain sense preserved. It is nothing less than a wicked waste of accumulated human strivings to sneer them out of existence. They will be found, every one of them, to have incarnated certain vital doctrines which it has cost centuries of toil and devotion properly to appreciate. Especially is this true of the Catholic faith, and if it were worth while, it might be shown how it is nothing less than a divine casket of precious remedies, and if it is to be brutally broken, it will take ages to rediscover and restore them. Of one thing I am certain, that their rediscovery and restoration will be necessary. I cannot too earnestly insist upon the need of our holding, each man for himself, by some faith which shall anchor him. It must not be taken up by chance. We must fight for it, for only so will it become OUR faith. The halt in indifference or in hostility is easy enough and seductive enough. The half-hearted thinks that when he has attained that stage he has completed the term of human wisdom. I say go on: do not stay there; do not take it for granted that there is nothing beyond; incessantly attempt an advance, and at last a light, dim it may be, will arise. It will not be a completed system, perfect in all points, an answer to all our questions, but at least it will give ground for hope.

We had to face the trials of our friends, and we had to face death. I do not say for an instant that we had any effectual reply to these great arguments against us. We never so much as sought for one, knowing how all men had sought and failed. But we were able to say there is some compensation, that there is another side, and this is all that man can say. No theory of the world is possible. The storm, the rain slowly rotting the harvest, children sickening in cellars are obvious; but equally obvious are an evening in June, the delight of men and women in one another, in music, and in the exercise of thought. There can surely be no question that the sum of satisfaction is increasing, not merely in the gross but for each human being, as the earth from which we sprang is being worked out of the race, and a higher type is being developed. I may observe, too, that although it is usually supposed, it is erroneously supposed, that it is pure doubt which disturbs or depresses us. Simple suspense is in fact very rare, for there are few persons so constituted as to be able to remain in it. It is dogmatism under the cloak of doubt which pulls us down. It is the dogmatism of death, for example, which we have to avoid. The open grave is dogmatic, and we say THAT MAN HAS GONE, but this is as much a transgression of the limits of certitude as if we were to say HE IS AN ANGEL IN BLISS. The proper attitude, the attitude enjoined by the severest exercise of the reason is, I DO NOT KNOW; and in this there is an element of hope, now rising and now falling, but always sufficient to prevent that blank despair which we must feel if we consider it as settled that when we lie down under the grass there is an absolute end.

The provision in nature of infinity ever present to us is an immense help. No man can look up to the stars at night and reflect upon what lies behind them without feeling that the tyranny of the senses is loosened, and the tyranny, too, of the conclusions of his logic. The beyond and the beyond, let us turn it over as we may, let us consider it as a child considers it, or by the light of the newest philosophy, is a constant, visible warning not to make our minds the measure of the universe. Underneath the stars what dreams, what conjectures arise, shadowy enough, it is true; but one thing we cannot help believing as irresistibly as if by geometrical deduction--that the sphere of that understanding of ours, whose function it seems to be to imprison us, is limited.

Going through a churchyard one afternoon I noticed that nearly all the people who were buried there, if the inscriptions on the tombstones might be taken to represent the thoughts of the departed when they were alive, had been intent solely on their own personal salvation. The question with them all seemed to have been, shall *I* go to heaven? Considering the tremendous difference between heaven and hell in the popular imagination, it was very natural that these poor creatures should be anxious above everything to know whether they would be in hell or heaven for ever. Surely, however, this is not the highest frame of mind, nor is it one to be encouraged. I would rather do all I can to get out of it, and to draw others out of it too. Our aim ought not so much to be the salvation of this poor petty self, but of that in me which alone makes it worth while to save me; of that alone which I hope will be saved, immortal truth. The very centre of the existence of the ordinary chapel-goer and church-goer needs to be shifted from self to what is outside self, and yet is truly self, and the sole truth of self. If the truth lives, WE live, and if it dies, we are dead. Our theology stands in need of a reformation greater than that of Luther's. It may be said that the attempt to replace the care for self in us by a care for the universal is ridiculous. Man cannot rise to that height. I do not believe it. I believe we can rise to it. Every ordinary unselfish act is a proof of the capacity to rise to it; and the mother's denial of all care for her own happiness, if she can but make her child happy, is a sublime anticipation. It may be called an instinct, but in the course of time it will be possible to develop a wider instinct in us, so that our love for the truth shall be even maternally passionate and self-forgetting.

After all our searching it was difficult to find anything which, in the case of a man like John the waiter, for example, could be of any service to him. At his age efficient help was beyond us, and in his case the problem presented itself in its simple nakedness. What comfort is there discoverable for the wretched which is not based upon illusion? We could not tell him that all he endured was right and proper. But even to him we were able to offer something. We did all we could to soothe him. On the Sunday, at least, he was able to find some relief from his labours, and he entered into a different region. He came to see us in the afternoon and evening occasionally, and brought his boy. Father and son were pulled up out of the vault, brought into the daylight, and led into an open expanse. We tried above everything to interest them, even in the smallest degree, in what is universal and impersonal, feeling that in that direction lies healing. We explained to the child as well as we could some morsels of science, and in explaining to him we explained to the father as well. When the anguish begotten by some outbreak on the part of the wife more violent than usual became almost too much to bear, we did our best to counsel, and as a last consolation we could point to Death, divine Death, and repose. It was but for a few more years at the utmost, and then must come a rest which no sorrow could invade. "Having death as an ally, I do not tremble at shadows," is an immortal quotation from some unknown Greek author. Providence, too, by no miracle, came to our relief. The wife died, as it was foreseen she must, and that weight being removed, some elasticity and recoil developed itself. John's one thought now was for his child, and by means of the child the father passed out of himself, and connected himself with the future. The child did in fact teach the father exactly what we tried to teach, and taught it with a power of conviction which never could have been produced by any mere appeals to the reason. The father felt that he was battered, useless, and a failure, but that in the boy there were unknown possibilities, and that he might in after life say that it was to this battered, useless failure of a father he owed his success. There was nothing now that he would not do to help Tom's education, and we joyfully aided as best we could. So, partly I believe by us, but far more by nature herself, John's salvation was wrought out at least in a measure; discord by the intervention of another note resolved itself into a kind of harmony, and even through the skylight in the Strand a glimpse of the azure was obtained.

I hope my readers, if I should ever have any, will remember that what I wish to do is to give some account of the manner in which we sought to be of service to the small and very humble circle of persons whom we had collected about us. I have preserved no record of anything; I am merely putting down what now comes into my mind--the two or three articles, not thirty-nine, nor, alas! a third of that number--which we were able to hold. I recollect one or two more which perhaps are worth preservation. In my younger days the aim of theologians was the justification of the ways of God to man. They could not succeed. They succeeded no better than ourselves in satisfying the intellect with a system. Nor does the Christian religion profess any such satisfaction. It teaches rather the great doctrine of a Remedy, of a Mediator; and therein it is profoundly true. It is unphilosophical in the sense that it offers no explanation from a single principle, and leaves the ultimate mystery as dark as before, but it is in accordance with our intuitions. Everywhere in nature we see exaction of penalties down to the uttermost farthing, but following after this we discern forgiveness, obliterating and restorative. Both tendencies exist. Nature is Rhadamanthine, and more so, for she visits the sins of the fathers upon the children; but there is in her also an infinite Pity, healing all wounds, softening all calamities, ever hastening to alleviate and repair. Christianity in strange historical fashion is an expression of nature, a projection of her into a biography and a creed.

We endeavoured to follow Christianity in the depth of its distinction between right and wrong. Herein this religion is of priceless value. Philosophy proclaims the unity of our nature. To philosophy every passion is as natural as every act of saintlike negation, and one of the usual effects of thinking or philosophising is to bring together all that is apparently contrary in man, and to show how it proceeds really from one centre. But Christianity had not to propound a theory of man; it had to redeem the world. It laid awful stress on the duality in us, and the stress laid on that duality is the world's salvation. The words right and wrong are not felt now as they were felt by Paul. They shade off one into the other. Nevertheless, if mankind is not to be lost, the ancient antagonism must be maintained. The shallowest of mortals is able now to laugh at the notion of a personal devil. No doubt there is no such thing existent; but the horror at evil which could find no other expression than in the creation of a devil is no subject for laughter, and if it do not in some shape or other survive, the race itself will not survive. No religion, so far as I know, has dwelt like Christianity with such profound earnestness on the bisection of man-

-on the distinction within him, vital to the very last degree, between the higher and the lower, heaven and hell. What utter folly is it because of an antique vesture to condemn as effete what the vesture clothes! Its doctrine and its sacred story are fixtures in concrete form of precious thoughts purchased by blood and tears.

I fancy I see the sneer of theologians and critics at our efforts. The theologians will mock us because we had nothing better to say. I can only reply that we did our best. We said all we knew, and we would most thankfully have said more, had we been sure that it must be true. I would remind, too, those of our judges who think that we were such wretched mortals, blind leaders of the blind, that there have been long ages during which men never pretended to understand more than we professed to understand. To say nothing of the Jews, whose meagre system would certainly not have been thought either satisfying or orthodox by modern Christians, the Greeks and Romans lived in no clearer light than that which shines on me. The critics, too, will condemn because of our weakness; but this defect I at once concede. The severest critic could not possibly be so severe as I am upon myself. I KNOW my failings. He, probably, would miss many of them. But, again I urge that men are not to be debarred by reason of weakness from doing what little good may lie within reach of their hands. Had we attempted to save scholars and thinkers we should have deserved the ridicule with which no doubt we shall be visited. We aspired to save nobody. We knew no salvation ourselves. We ventured humbly to bring a feeble ray of light into the dwellings of two or three poor men and women; and if Prometheus, fettered to his rock, dwelt with pride on the blind hopes which he had caused to visit mortals, the hopes which "stopped the continued anticipation of their destiny," we perhaps may be pardoned if at times we thought that what we were doing was not altogether vanity.

CHAPTER VII--QUI DEDIT IN MARI VIAM

From time to time I received a newspaper from my native town, and one morning, looking over the advertisements, I caught sight of one which arrested me. It was as follows:-

"A Widow Lady desires a situation as Daily Governess to little children. Address E. B., care of Mrs. George Andrews, Fancy Bazaar, High Street."

Mrs. George Andrews was a cousin of Ellen Butts, and that this was her advertisement I had not the slightest doubt. Suddenly, without being able to give the least reason for it, an unconquerable desire to see her arose within me. I could not understand it. I recollected that memorable resolution after Miss Arbour's story years ago. How true that counsel of Miss Arbour's was! and yet it had the defect of most counsel. It was but a principle; whether it suited this particular case was the one important point on which Miss Arbour was no authority. What WAS it which prompted this inexplicable emotion? A thousand things rushed through my head without reason or order. I begin to believe that a first love never dies. A boy falls in love at eighteen or nineteen. The attachment comes to nothing. It is broken off for a multitude of reasons, and he sees its absurdity. He marries afterwards some other woman whom he even adores, and he has children for whom he spends his life; yet in an obscure corner of his soul he preserves everlastingly the cherished picture of the girl who first was dear to him. She, too, marries. In process of time she is fifty years old, and he is fifty-two. He has not seen her for thirty years or more, but he continually turns aside into the little oratory, to gaze upon the face as it last appeared to him when he left her at her gate and saw her no more. He inquires now and then timidly about her whenever he gets the chance. And once in his life he goes down to the town where she lives, solely in order to get a sight of her without her knowing anything about it. He does not succeed, and he comes back and tells his wife, from whom he never conceals any secrets, that he has been away on business. I did not for a moment confess that my love for Ellen had returned. I knew who she was and what she was, and what had led to our separation; but nevertheless, all this obstinately remained in the background, and all the passages of love between us, all our kisses, and above everything, her tears at that parting in her father's house, thrust themselves upon me. It was a mystery to me. What should have induced that utterly unexpected resurrection of what I believed to be dead and buried, is beyond my comprehension. However, the fact remains. I did not to myself admit that this was love, but it WAS love, and that it should have shot up with such swift vitality merely because I had happened to see those initials was miraculous. I pretended to myself that I should like once more to see Mrs. Butts- -perhaps she might be in want and I could help her. I shrank from writing to her or from making myself known to her, and at last I hit upon the expedient of answering her advertisement in a feigned name, and requesting her to call at the King's Arms hotel upon a gentleman who wished to engage a widow lady to teach his children. To prevent any previous inquiries on her part, I said that my name was Williams, that I lived in the country at some little distance from the town, but that I should be there on business on the day named. I took up my quarters at the King's Arms the night before. It seemed very strange to be in an inn in the place in which I was born. I retired early to my bedroom, and looked out in the clear moonlight over the river. The landscape seemed haunted by ghosts of my former self. At one particular point, so well known, I stood fishing. At another, equally well known, where the water was dangerously deep, I was examining the ice; and round the corner was the boathouse where we kept the little craft in which I had voyaged so many hundreds of miles on excursions upwards beyond where the navigation ends, or, still more fascinating, down to where the water widens and sails are to be seen, and there is a foretaste of the distant sea. It is no pleasure to me to revisit scenes in which earlier days have been passed. I detest the sentimental melancholy which steals over me; the sense of the lapse of time, and the reflection that so many whom I knew are dead. I would always, if possible, spend my holiday in some new scene, fresh to me, and full of new interest. I slept but little, and when the morning came, instead of carrying out my purpose of wandering through the streets, I was so sick of the mood by which I had been helplessly overcome, that I sat at a distance from the window in the coffee-room, and read diligently last week's Bell's Weekly Messenger. My reading, however, was nothing. I do not suppose I comprehended the simplest paragraph. My thoughts were away, and I watched the clock slowly turning towards the hour when Ellen was to call. I foresaw that I should not be able to speak to her at the inn. If I have anything particular to say to anybody, I can always say it so much better out of doors. I dreaded the confinement of the room, and the necessity for looking into her face. Under the sky, and in motion, I should be more at liberty. At last eleven struck from the church in the square, and five minutes afterwards the waiter entered to announce Mrs. Butts. I was therefore right, and she was "E. B." I was sure that I should not be recognised. Since I saw her last I had grown a beard, my hair had got a little grey, and she was always a little short-sighted. She came in, and as she entered she put away over her bonnet her thick black veil. Not ten seconds passed before she was seated on the opposite side of the table to that on which I was sitting, but I re- read in her during those ten seconds the whole history of years. I cannot say that externally she looked worn or broken. I had imagined that I should see her undone with her great troubles, but to some extent, and yet not altogether, I was mistaken. The cheek-bones were more prominent than of old, and her dark-brown hair drawn tightly over her forehead increased the clear paleness of the face; the just perceptible tint of colour which I recollect being now altogether withdrawn. But she was not haggard, and evidently not vanquished. There was even a gaiety on her face, perhaps a trifle enforced, and although the darkness of sorrow gleamed behind it, the sorrow did not seem to be ultimate, but to be in front of a final background, if not of joy, at least of resignation. Her ancient levity of manner had vanished, or at most had left nothing but a trace. I thought I detected it here and there in a line about the mouth, and perhaps in her walk. There was a reminiscence of it too in her clothes. Notwithstanding poverty and distress, the old neatness--that particular care which used to charm me so when I was little more than a child, was there still. I was always susceptible to this virtue, and delicate hands and feet, with delicate care bestowed thereon, were more attractive to me than slovenly beauty. I noticed that the gloves, though mended, fitted with the same precision, and that her dress was unwrinkled and perfectly graceful. Whatever she might have had to endure, it had not destroyed that self-centred satisfaction which makes life tolerable.

I was impelled at once to say that I had to beg her pardon for asking her there. Unfortunately I was obliged to go over to Cowston, a village which was about three miles from the town. Perhaps she would not mind walking part of the way with me through the meadows, and then we could talk with more freedom, as I should not feel pressed for time. To this arrangement she at once agreed, and dropping her thick veil over her face, we went out. In a few minutes we were clear of the houses, and I began the conversation.

"Have you been in the habit of teaching?"

"No. The necessity for taking to it has only lately arisen."

"What can you teach?"

"Not much beyond what children of ten or eleven years old are expected to know; but I could take charge of them entirely."

"Have you any children of your own?"

"One."

"Could you take a situation as resident teacher if you have a child?"

"I must get something to do, and if I can make no arrangement by which my child can live with me, I shall try and place her with a friend. I may be able to hear of some appointment as a daily governess."

"I should have thought that in your native town you would have been easily able to find employment--you must be well known?"

There was a pause, and after a moment or so she said:-

"We were well known once, but we went abroad and lost all our money. My husband died abroad. When I returned, I found that there was very little which my friends could do for me. I am not accomplished, and there are crowds of young women who are more capable than I am. Moreover, I saw that I was becoming a burden, and people called on me rather as a matter of duty than for any other reason. You don't know how soon all but the very best insensibly neglect very poor relatives if they are not gifted or attractive. I do not wonder at being made to feel this, nor do I blame anybody. My little girl is a cripple, my rooms are dull, and I have nothing in me with which to amuse or entertain visitors. Pardon my going into this detail. It was necessary to say something in order to explain my position."

"May I ask what salary you will require if you live in the house?"

"Five-and-thirty pounds a year, but I might take less if I were asked to do so."

"Are you a member of the Church of England?"

"No."

"To what religious body do you belong?"

"I am an Independent, but I would go to Church if my employers wished it."

"I thought the Independents objected to go to Church."

"They do; but I should not object, if I could hear anything at the Church which would help me."

"I am rather surprised at your indifference."

"I was once more particular, but I have seen much suffering, and some things which were important to me are not so now, and others which were not important have become so."

I then made up a little story. My sister and I lived together. We were about to take up our abode at Cowston, but were as yet strangers to it. I was left a widower with two little children whom my sister could not educate, as she could not spare the time. She would naturally have selected the governess herself, but she was at some distance. She would like to see Mrs. Butts before engaging her finally, but she thought that as this advertisement presented itself, I might make some preliminary inquiries. Perhaps, however, now that Mrs. Butts knew the facts, she would object to living in the house. I put it in this way, feeling sure that she would catch my meaning.

"I am afraid that this situation will not suit me. I could not go backwards and forwards so far every day."

"I understand you perfectly, and feared that this would be your decision. But if you hesitate, I can give you the best of references. I had not thought of that before. References of course will be required by you as well as by me."

I put my hand in my pocket for my pocket-book, but I could not find it. We had now reached a part of our road familiar enough to both of us. Along that very path Ellen and I had walked years ago. Under those very trees, on that very seat had we sat, and she and I were there again. All the old confidences, confessions, tendernesses, rushed upon me. What is there which is more potent than the recollection of past love to move us to love, and knit love with closest bonds? Can we ever cease to love the souls who have once shared all that we know and feel? Can we ever be indifferent to those who have our secrets, and whose secrets we hold? As I looked at her, I remembered what she knew about me, and what I knew about her, and this simple thought so overmastered me, that I could hold out no longer. I said to her that if she would like to rest for one moment, I might be able to find my papers. We sat down together, and she drew up her veil to read the address which I was about to give her. She glanced at me, as I thought, with a strange expression of excited interrogation, and something swiftly passed across her face, which warned me that I had not a moment to lose. I took out one of my own cards, handed it to her, and said, "Here is a reference which perhaps you may know." She bent over it, turned to me, fixed her eyes intently and directly on mine for one moment, and then I thought she would have fallen. My arm was around her in an instant, her head was on my shoulder, and my many wanderings were over. It was broad, high, sunny noon, the most solitary hour of the daylight in those fields. We were roused by the distant sound of the town clock striking twelve; we rose and went on together to Cowston by the river bank, returning late in the evening.

CHAPTER VIII--FLAGELLUM NON APPROQUINABIT TABERNACULO TUO

I suppose that the reason why in novels the story ends with a marriage is partly that the excitement of the tale ceases then, and partly also because of a theory that marriage is an epoch, determining the career of life after it. The epoch once announced, nothing more need be explained; everything else follows as a matter of course. These notes of mine are autobiographical, and not a romance. I have never known much about epochs. I have had one or two, one specially when I first began to read and think; but after that, if I have changed, it has been slowly and imperceptibly. My life, therefore, is totally unfitted to be the basis of fiction. My return to Ellen, and our subsequent marriage, were only partially an epoch. A change had come, but it was one which had long been preparing. Ellen's experiences had altered her position, and mine too was altered. She had been driven into religion by trouble, and knowing nothing of criticism or philosophy, retained the old forms for her religious feeling. But the very quickness of her emotion caused her to welcome all new and living modes of expressing it. It is only when feeling has ceased to accompany a creed that it becomes fixed, and verbal departures from it are counted heresy. I too cared less for argument, and it even gave me pleasure to talk in her dialect, so familiar to me, but for so many years unused.

It was now necessary for me to add to my income. I had nothing upon which to depend save my newspaper, which was obviously insufficient. At last, I succeeded in obtaining some clerical employment. For no other work was I fit, for my training had not been special in any one direction. My hours were long, from ten in the morning till seven in the evening, and as I was three miles distant from the office, I was really away from home for eleven hours every day, excepting on Sundays. I began to calculate that my life consisted of nothing but the brief spaces allowed to me for rest, and these brief spaces I could not enjoy because I dwelt upon their brevity. There was some excuse for me. Never could there be any duty incumbent upon man much more inhuman and devoid of interest than my own. How often I thought about my friend Clark, and his experiences became mine. The whole day I did nothing but write, and what I wrote called forth no single faculty of the mind. Nobody who has not tried such an occupation can possibly forecast the strange habits, humours, fancies, and diseases which after a time it breeds. I was shut up in a room half below the ground. In this room were three other men besides myself, two of them between fifty and sixty, and one about three or four-and-twenty. All four of us kept books or copied letters from ten to seven, with an interval of three-quarters of an hour for dinner. In all three of these men, as in the case of Clark's companions, there had been developed, partly I suppose by the circumstance of enforced idleness of brain, the most loathsome tendency to obscenity. This was the one subject which was common ground, and upon which they could talk. It was fostered too by a passion for beer, which was supplied by the publican across the way, who was perpetually travelling to and fro with cans. My horror when I first found out into what society I was thrust was unspeakable. There was a clock within a hundred yards of my window which struck the hours and quarters. How I watched that clock! My spirits rose or fell with each division of the day. From ten to twelve there was nothing but gloom. By half-past twelve I began to discern dinner time, and the prospect was brighter. After dinner there was nothing to be done but doggedly to endure until five, and at five I was able to see over the distance from five to seven. My disgust at my companions, however, came to be mixed with pity. I found none of them cruel, and I received many little kindnesses from them. I discovered that their trade was largely answerable for the impurity of thought and speech which so shocked me. Its monotony compelled some countervailing stimulus, and as they had never been educated to care for anything in particular, they found the necessary relief in sensuality. At first they "chaffed" and worried me a good deal because of my silence, but at last they began to think I was "religious," and then they ceased to torment me. I rather encouraged them in the belief that I had a right to exemption from their conversation, and I passed, I believe, for a Plymouth brother. The only thing which they could not comprehend was that I made no attempt to convert them.

The whole establishment was under the rule of a deputy-manager, who was the terror of the place. He was tall, thin, and suffered occasionally from spitting of blood, brought on no doubt from excitement. He was the strangest mixture of exactitude and passion. He had complete mastery over every detail of the business, and he never blundered. All his work was thorough, down to the very bottom, and he had the most intolerant hatred of everything which was loose and inaccurate. He never passed a day without flaming out into oaths and curses against his subordinates, and they could not say in his wildest fury that his ravings were beside the mark. He was wrong in his treatment of men--utterly wrong--but his facts were always correct. I never saw anybody hated as he was, and the hatred against him was the more intense because nobody could convict him of a mistake. He seemed to enjoy a storm, and knew nothing whatever of the constraints which with ordinary men prevent abusive and brutal language to those around them. Some of his clerks suffered greatly from him, and he almost broke down two or three from the constant nervous strain upon them produced by fear of his explosions. For my own part, although I came in for a full share of his temper, I at once made up my mind as soon as I discovered what he was, not to open my lips to him except under compulsion. My one object now was to get a living. I wished also to avoid the self-mortification which must ensue from altercation. I dreaded, as I have always dreaded beyond what I can tell, the chaos and wreck which, with me, follows subjugation by anger, and I held to my resolve under all provocation. It was very difficult, but how many times I have blessed myself for adhesion to it. Instead of going home undone with excitement, and trembling with fear of dismissal, I have walked out of my dungeon having had to bite my lips till the blood came, but still conqueror, and with peace of mind.

Another stratagem of defence which I adopted at the office was never to betray to a soul anything about myself. Nobody knew anything about me, whether I was married or single, where I lived, or what I thought upon a single subject of any importance. I cut off my office life in this way from my life at home so completely that I was two selves, and my true self was not stained by contact with my other self. It was a comfort to me to think the moment the clock struck seven that my second self died, and that my first self suffered nothing by having anything to do with it. I was not the person who sat at the desk downstairs and endured the abominable talk of his colleagues and the ignominy of serving such a chief. I knew nothing about him. I was a citizen walking London streets; I had my opinions upon human beings and books; I was on equal terms with my friends; I was Ellen's husband; I was, in short, a man. By this scrupulous isolation, I preserved myself, and the clerk was not debarred from the domain of freedom.

It is very terrible to think that the labour by which men are to live should be of this order. The ideal of labour is that it should be something in which we can take an interest and even a pride. Immense masses of it in London are the merest slavery, and it is as mechanical as the daily journey of the omnibus horse. There is no possibility of relieving it, and all the ordinary copybook advice of moralists and poets as to the temper in which we should earn our bread is childish nonsense. If a man is a painter, or a physician, or a barrister, or even a tradesman, well and good. The maxims of authors may be of some service to him, and he may be able to exemplify them; but if he is a copying clerk they are an insult, and he can do nothing but arch his back to bear his burden and find some compensation elsewhere. True it is, that beneficent Nature here, as always, is helpful. Habit, after a while, mitigated much of the bitterness of destiny. The hard points of the flint became smoothed and worn away by perpetual tramping over them, so that they no longer wounded with their original sharpness; and the sole of the foot was in time provided with a merciful callosity. Then, too, there was developed an appetite which was voracious for all that was best. Who shall tell the revulsion on reaching home, which I should never have known had I lived a life of idleness! Ellen was fond of hearing me read, and with a little care I was able to select what would bear reading--dramas, for example. She liked the reading for the reading's sake, and she liked to know that what I thought was communicated to her; that she was not excluded from the sphere in which I lived. Of the office she never heard a word, and I never would tell her anything about it; but there was scarcely a single book in my possession which could be read aloud, that we did not go through together in this way. I don't prescribe this kind of life to everybody. Some of my best friends, I know, would find it intolerable, but it suited us. Philosophy and religion I did not touch. It was necessary to choose themes with varying human interest, such as the best works of fiction, a play, or a poem; and these perhaps, on the whole, did me more good at that time than speculation. Oh, how many times have I left my office humiliated by some silently endured outbreak on the part of my master, more galling because I could not put it aside as altogether gratuitous; and in less than an hour it was two miles away, and I was myself again. If a man wants to know what the potency of love is, he must be a menial; he must be despised. Those who are prosperous and courted cannot understand its power. Let him come home after he has suffered what is far worse than hatred--the contempt of a superior, who knows that he can afford to be contemptuous, seeing that he can replace his slave at a moment's notice. Let him be trained by his tyrant to dwell upon the thought that he belongs to the vast crowd of people in London who are unimportant; almost useless; to whom it is a charity to offer employment; who are conscious of possessing no gift which makes them of any value to anybody, and he will then comprehend the divine efficacy of the affection of that woman to whom he is dear. God's mercy be praised ever more for it! I cannot write poetry, but if I could, no theme would tempt me like that of love to such a person as I was--not love, as I say again, to the hero, but love to the Helot. Over and over again, when I have thought about it, I have felt my poor heart swell with a kind of uncontrollable fervour. I have often, too, said to myself that this love is no delusion. If we were to set it down as nothing more than a merciful cheat on the part of the Creator, however pleasant it might be, it would lose its charm. If I were to think that my wife's devotion to me is nothing more than the simple expression of a necessity to love somebody, that there is nothing in me which justifies such devotion, I should be miserable. Rather, I take it, is the love of woman to man a revelation of the relationship in which God stands to him--of what OUGHT to be, in fact. In the love of a woman to the man who is of no account God has provided us with a true testimony of what is in His own heart. I often felt this when looking at myself and at Ellen. "What is there in me?" I have said, "is she not the victim of some self-created deception?" and I was wretched till I considered that in her I saw the Divine Nature itself, and that her passion was a stream straight from the Highest. The love of woman is, in other words, a living witness never failing of an actuality in God which otherwise we should never know. This led me on to connect it with Christianity; but I am getting incoherent and must stop.

My employment now was so incessant, for it was still necessary that I should write for my newspaper--although my visits to the House of Commons had perforce ceased--that I had no time for any schemes or dreams such as those which had tormented me when I had more leisure. In one respect this was a blessing. Destiny now had prescribed for me. I was no longer agitated by ignorance of what I ought to do. My present duty was obviously to get my own living, and having got that, I could do little besides save continue the Sundays with M'Kay.

We were almost entirely alone. We had no means of making any friends. We had no money, and no gifts of any kind. We were neither of us witty nor attractive, but I have often wondered, nevertheless, what it was which prevented us from obtaining acquaintance with persons who thronged to houses in which I could see nothing worth a twopenny omnibus fare. Certain it is, that we went out of our way sometimes to induce people to call upon us whom we thought we should like; but, if they came once or twice, they invariably dropped off, and we saw no more of them. This behaviour was so universal that, without the least affectation, I acknowledge there must be something repellent in me, but what it is I cannot tell. That Ellen was the cause of the general aversion, it is impossible to believe. The only theory I have is, that partly owing to a constant sense of fatigue, due to imperfect health, and partly to chafing irritation at mere gossip, although I had no power to think of anything better, or say anything better myself, I was avoided both by the commonplace and those who had talent. Commonplace persons avoided me because I did not chatter, and persons of talent because I stood for nothing. "There was nothing in me." We met at M'Kay's two gentlemen whom we thought we might invite to our house. One of them was an antiquarian. He had discovered in an excavation in London some Roman remains. This had led him on to the study of the position and boundaries of the Roman city. He had become an authority upon this subject, and had lectured upon it. He came; but as we were utterly ignorant, and could not, with all our efforts, manifest any sympathy which he valued at the worth of a pin, he soon departed, and departed for ever. The second was a student of Elizabethan literature, and I rashly concluded at once that he must be most delightful. He likewise came. I showed him my few poor books, which he condemned, and I found that such observations as I could make he considered as mere twaddle. I knew nothing, or next to nothing, about the editions or the curiosities, or the proposed emendations of obscure passages, and he, too, departed abruptly. I began to think after he had gone that my study of Shakespeare was mere dilettantism but I afterwards came to the conclusion that if a man wishes to spoil himself for Shakespeare, the best thing he can do is to turn Shakespearian critic.

My worst enemy at this time was ill health, and it was more distressing than it otherwise would have been, because I had such responsibilities upon me. When I lived alone I knew that if anything should happen to me it would be of no particular consequence, but now whenever I felt sick I was anxious on account of Ellen. What would become of her--this was the thought which kept me awake night after night when the terrors of depression were upon me, as they often were. But still, terrors with growing years had lost their ancient strength. My brain and nerves were quiet compared with what they were in times gone by, and I had gradually learned the blessed lesson which is taught by familiarity with sorrow, that the greater part of what is dreadful in it lies in the imagination. The true Gorgon head is seldom seen in reality. That it exists I do not doubt, but it is not so commonly visible as we think. Again, as we get older we find that all life is given us on conditions of uncertainty, and yet we walk courageously on. The labourer marries and has children, when there is nothing but his own strength between him and ruin. A million chances are encountered every day, and any one of the million accidents which might happen would cripple him or kill him, and put into the workhouse those who depend upon him. Yet he treads his path undisturbed. Life to all of us is a narrow plank placed across a gulf, which yawns on either side, and if we were perpetually looking down into it we should fall. So at last, the possibility of disaster ceased to affright me. I had been brought off safely so many times when destruction seemed imminent, that I grew hardened, and lay down quietly at night, although the whim of a madman might to-morrow cast me on the pavement. Frequently, as I have said, I could not do this, but I strove to do it, and was able to do it when in health.

I tried to think about nothing which expressed whatever in the world may be insoluble or simply tragic. A great change is just beginning to come over us in this respect. So many books I find are written which aim merely at new presentation of the hopeless. The contradictions of fate, the darkness of death, the fleeting of man over this brief stage of existence, whence we know not, and whither we know not, are favourite subjects with writers who seem to think that they are profound, because they can propose questions which cannot be answered. There is really more strength of mind required for resolving the commonest difficulty than is necessary for the production of poems on these topics. The characteristic of so much that is said and written now is melancholy; and it is melancholy, not because of any deeper acquaintance with the secrets of man than that which was possessed by our forefathers, but because it is easy to be melancholy, and the time lacks strength.

As I am now setting down, without much order or connection, the lessons which I had to learn, I may perhaps be excused if I add one or two others. I can say of them all, that they are not book lessons. They have been taught me by my own experience, and as a rule I have always found that in my own most special perplexities I got but little help from books or other persons. I had to find out for myself what was for me the proper way of dealing with them.

My love for Ellen was great, but I discovered that even such love as this could not be left to itself. It wanted perpetual cherishing. The lamp, if it was to burn brightly, required daily trimming, for people became estranged and indifferent, not so much by open quarrel or serious difference, as by the intervention of trifles which need but the smallest, although continuous effort for their removal. The true wisdom is to waste no time over them, but to eject them at once. Love, too, requires that the two persons who love one another shall constantly present to one another what is best in them, and to accomplish this, deliberate purpose, and even struggle, are necessary. If through relapse into idleness we do not attempt to bring soul and heart into active communion day by day, what wonder if this once exalted relationship become vulgar and mean?

I was much overworked. It was not the work itself which was such a trial, but the time it consumed. At best, I had but a clear space of an hour, or an hour and a half at home, and to slave merely for this seemed such a mockery! Day after day sped swiftly by, made up of nothing but this infernal drudgery, and I said to myself--Is this life? But I made up my mind that NEVER WOULD I GIVE MYSELF TONGUE. I clapped a muzzle on my mouth. Had I followed my own natural bent, I should have become expressive about what I had to endure, but I found that expression reacts on him who expresses and intensifies what is expressed. If we break out into rhetoric over a toothache, the pangs are not the easier, but the worse to be borne.

I naturally contracted a habit of looking forward from the present moment to one beyond. The whole week seemed to exist for the Sunday. On Monday morning I began counting the hours till Sunday should arrive. The consequence was, that

when it came, it was not enjoyed properly, and I wasted it in noting the swiftness of
its flight. Oh, how absurd is man! If we were to reckon up all the moments which
we really enjoy for their own sake, how few should we find them to be! The greatest part, far the greatest part, of our lives is spent in dreaming over the morrow, and
when it comes, it, too, is consumed in the anticipation of a brighter morrow, and so
the cheat is prolonged, even to the grave. This tendency, unconquerable though it
may appear to be, can to a great extent at any rate, be overcome by strenuous discipline. I tried to blind myself to the future, and many and many a time, as I walked
along that dreary New Road or Old St. Pancras Road, have I striven to compel myself not to look at the image of Hampstead Heath or Regent's Park, as yet six days in
front of me, but to get what I could out of what was then with me.

The instinct which leads us perpetually to compare what we are with what we
might be is no doubt of enormous value, and is the spring which prompts all action,
but, like every instinct, it is the source of greatest danger. I remember the day and
the very spot on which it flashed into me, like a sudden burst of the sun's rays, that
I had no right to this or that--to so much happiness, or even so much virtue. What
title-deeds could I show for such a right? Straightway it seemed as if the centre of a
whole system of dissatisfaction were removed, and as if the system collapsed. God,
creating from His infinite resources a whole infinitude of beings, had created me
with a definite position on the scale, and that position only could I claim. Cease the
trick of contrast. If I can by any means get myself to consider myself alone without
reference to others, discontent will vanish. I walk this Old St. Pancras Road on
foot-- another rides. Keep out of view him who rides and all persons riding, and
I shall not complain that I tramp in the wet. So also when I think how small and
weak I am.

How foolish it is to try and cure by argument what time will cure so completely
and so gently if left to itself. As I get older, the anxiety to prove myself right if I
quarrel dies out. I hold my tongue and time vindicates me, if it is possible to vindi-
cate me, or convicts me if I am wrong. Many and many a debate too which I have
had with myself alone has been settled in the same way. The question has been
put aside and has lost its importance. The ancient Church thought, and seriously
enough, no doubt, that all the vital interests of humanity were bound up with the
controversies upon the Divine nature; but the centuries have rolled on, and who

cares for those controversies now. The problems of death and immortality once upon a time haunted me so that I could hardly sleep for thinking about them. I cannot tell how, but so it is, that at the present moment, when I am years nearer the end, they trouble me but very little. If I could but bury and let rot things which torment me and come to no settlement--if I could always do this--what a blessing it would be.

CHAPTER IX--HOLIDAYS

I have said that Ellen had a child by her first husband. Marie, for that was her name, was now ten years old. She was like neither her mother nor father, and yet was SHOT as it were with strange gleams which reminded me of her paternal grandmother for a moment, and then disappeared. She had rather coarse dark hair, small black eyes, round face, and features somewhat blunt or blurred, the nose in particular being so. She had a tendency to be stout. For books she did not care, and it was with the greatest difficulty we taught her to read. She was not orderly or careful about her person, and in this respect was a sore disappointment--not that she was positively careless, but she took no pride in dress, nor in keeping her room and her wardrobe neat. She was fond of bright colours, which was another trial to Ellen, who disliked any approach to gaudiness. She was not by any means a fool, and she had a peculiarly swift mode of expressing herself upon persons and things. A stranger looking at her would perhaps have adjudged her inclined to sensuousness, and dull. She was neither one nor the other. She ate little, although she was fond of sweets. Her rather heavy face, with no clearly cut outline in it, was not the typical face for passion; but she was capable of passion to an extraordinary degree, and what is more remarkable, it was not explosive passion, or rather it was not passion which she suffered to explode. I remember once when she was a little mite she was asked out somewhere to tea. She was dressed and ready, but it began to rain fast, and she was told she could not go. She besought, but it was in vain. We could not afford cabs, and there was no omnibus. Marie, finding all her entreaties were useless, quietly walked out of the room; and after some little time her mother, calling her and finding she did not come, went to look for her. She had gone into the back-yard, and was sitting there in the rain by the side of the water-butt. She was soaked, and her best clothes were spoiled. I must confess that I did not take very kindly to her. I was irritated at her slowness in learning; it was, in fact, painful to be obliged to teach her. I thought that perhaps she might have some undeveloped taste for music, but she showed none, and our attempts to get her to sing ordinary melodies were a failure. She was more or less of a locked cabinet to me. I tried her with the two or three keys which I had, but finding that none of them fitted, I took no more pains about her.

One Sunday we determined upon a holiday. It was a bold adventure for us, but we had made up our minds. There was an excursion train to Hastings, and accordingly Ellen, Marie, and myself were at London Bridge Station early in the morning. It was a lovely summer's day in mid-July. The journey down was uncomfortable enough in consequence of the heat and dust, but we heeded neither one nor the other in the hope of seeing the sea. We reached Hastings at about eleven o'clock, and strolled westwards towards Bexhill. Our pleasure was exquisite. Who can tell, save the imprisoned Londoner, the joy of walking on the clean sea-sand! What a delight that was, to say nothing of the beauty of the scenery! To be free of the litter and filth of a London suburb, of its broken hedges, its brickbats, its torn advertisements, its worn and trampled grass in fields half given over to the speculative builder: in place of this, to tread the immaculate shore over which breathed a wind not charged with soot; to replace the dull, shrouding obscurity of the smoke by a distance so distinct that the masts of the ships whose hulls were buried below the horizon were visible--all this was perfect bliss. It was not very poetic bliss, perhaps; but nevertheless it is a fact that the cleanness of the sea and the sea air was as attractive to us as any of the sea attributes. We had a wonderful time. Only in the country is it possible to note the change of morning into mid-day, of mid-day into afternoon, and of afternoon into evening; and it is only in the country, therefore, that a day seems stretched out into its proper length. We had brought all our food with us, and sat upon the shore in the shadow of a piece of the cliff. A row of heavy white clouds lay along the horizon almost unchangeable and immovable, with their summit-lines and the part of the mass just below them steeped in sunlight. The level opaline water differed only from a floor by a scarcely perceptible heaving motion, which broke into the faintest of ripples at our feet. So still was the great ocean, so quietly did everything lie in it, that the wavelets which licked the beach were as pure and bright as if they were a part of the mid-ocean depths. About a mile from us, at one o'clock, a long row of porpoises appeared, showing themselves in graceful curves for half-an-hour or so, till they went out farther to sea off Fairlight. Some fishing- boats were becalmed just in front of us. Their shadows slept, or almost slept, upon the water, a gentle quivering alone showing that it was not complete sleep, or if sleep, that it was sleep with dreams. The intensity of the sunlight sharpened the outlines of every little piece of rock, and of the pebbles, in a manner which seemed supernatural to us Londoners. In London we get the heat of the sun, but not his light, and the separation of individual parts into such vivid isolation was so surprising that even Marie noticed it, and said it "all seemed as if she were looking through a glass." It was perfect--perfect in its beauty--and perfect because, from the sun in the heavens down to the fly with burnished wings on the hot rock, there was nothing out of harmony. Everything breathed one spirit. Marie played near us; Ellen and I sat still, doing nothing. We wanted nothing, we had nothing to achieve; there were no curiosities to be seen, there was no particular place to be reached, no "plan of operations," and London was forgotten for the time. It lay behind us in the north-west, and the cliff was at the back of us shutting out all thought of it. No reminiscences and no anticipations disturbed us; the present was sufficient, and occupied us totally.

I should like, if I could, to write an essay upon the art of enjoying a holiday. It is sad to think how few people know how to enjoy one, although they are so precious. We do not sufficiently consider that enjoyment of every kind is an art carefully to be learnt, and specially the art of making the most of a brief space set apart for pleasure. It is foolish, for example, if a man, city bred, has but twelve hours before him, to spend more of it in eating and drinking than is necessary. Eating and drinking produce stupidity, at least in some degree, which may just as well be reserved for town. It is foolish also to load the twelve hours with a task--so much to be done. The sick person may perhaps want exercise, but to the tolerably healthy the best of all recreation is the freedom from fetters even when they are self-imposed.

Our train homewards was due at Bexhill a little after seven. By five o'clock a change gradual but swift was observed. The clouds which had charmed us all through the morning and afternoon were in reality thunder-clouds, which woke up like a surprised army under perfect discipline, and moved magnificently towards us. Already afar off we heard the softened echoing roll of the thunder. Every now and then we saw a sharp thrust of lightning down into the water, and shuddered when we thought that perhaps underneath that stab there might be a ship with living men. The battle at first was at such a distance that we watched it with intense and solemn delight. As yet not a breath of air stirred, but presently, over in the south-east, a dark ruffled patch appeared on the horizon, and we agreed that it was time to go. The indistinguishable continuous growl now became articulated into distinct crashes. I had miscalculated the distance to the station, and before we got there the rain, skirmishing in advance, was upon us. We took shelter in a cottage for a moment in order that Ellen might get a glass of water--bad-looking stuff it was, but she was very thirsty--and put on her cloak. We then started again on our way. We reached the station at about half-past six, before the thunder was overhead, but not before Ellen had got wet, despite all my efforts to protect her. She was also very hot from hurrying, and yet there was nothing to be done but to sit in a kind of covered shed till the train came up. The thunder and lightning were, however, so tremendous, that we thought of nothing else. When they were at their worst, the lightning looked like the upset of a cauldron of white glowing metal--with such strength, breadth, and volume did it descend. Just as the train arrived, the roar began to abate, and in about half-an-hour it had passed over to the north, leaving behind the rain, cold and continuous, which fell all round us from a dark, heavy, grey sky. The carnage in which we were was a third-class, with seats arranged parallel to the sides. It was crowded, and we were obliged to sit in the middle, exposed to the draught which the tobacco smoke made necessary. Some of the company were noisy, and before we got to Red Hill became noisier, as the brandy-flasks which had been well filled at Hastings began to work. Many were drenched, and this was an excuse for much of the drinking; although for that matter, any excuse or none is generally sufficient. At Red Hill we were stopped by other trains, and before we came to Croydon we were an hour late. We had now become intolerably weary. The songs were disgusting, and some of the women who were with the men had also been drinking, and behaved in a manner which it was not pleasant that Ellen and Marie should see. The carriage was lighted fortunately by one dim lamp only which hung in the middle, and I succeeded at last in getting seats at the further end, where there was a knot of more decent persons who had huddled up there away from the others. All the glory of the morning was forgotten. Instead of three happy, exalted creatures, we were three dejected, shivering mortals, half poisoned with foul air and the smell of spirits. We crawled up to London Bridge at the slowest pace, and, finally, the railway company discharged us on the platform at ten minutes past eleven. Not a place in any omnibus could be secured, and we therefore walked for a mile or so till I saw a cab, which--unheard-of expense for me--I engaged, and we were landed at our own house exactly at half-past twelve. The first thing to be done was to get Marie to bed. She was instantly asleep, and was none the worse for her journey. With Ellen the case was different. She could not sleep, and the next morning was feverish. She insisted that it was nothing more than a bad cold, and would on no account permit me even to give her any medicine. She would get up presently, and she and Marie could get on well enough together. But when I reached home on Monday evening, Ellen was worse, and was still in bed.

I sent at once for the doctor, who would give no opinion for a day or two, but meanwhile directed that she was to remain where she was, and take nothing but the lightest food. Tuesday night passed, and the fever still increased. I had become very anxious, but I dared not stay with her, for I knew not what might happen if I were absent from my work. I was obliged to try and think of somebody who would come and help us. Our friend Taylor, who once was the coal-porter at Somerset House, came into my mind. He, as I have said when talking about him, was married, but had no children. To him accordingly I went. I never shall forget the alacrity with which he prompted his wife to go, and with which she consented. I was shut up in my own sufferings, but I remember a flash of joy that all our efforts in our room had not been in vain. I was delighted that I had secured assistance, but I do believe the uppermost thought was delight that we had been able to develop gratitude and affection. Mrs. Taylor was an "ordinary woman." She was about fifty, rather stout, and entirely uneducated. But when she took charge at our house, all her best qualities found expression. It is true enough, omnium consensu capax imperii nisi imperasset, but it is equally true that under the pressure of trial and responsibility we are often stronger than when there is no pressure. Many a man will acknowledge that in difficulty he has surprised himself by a resource and coolness which he never suspected before. Mrs. Taylor I always thought to be rather weak and untrustworthy, but I found that when WEIGHT was placed upon her, she was steady as a rock, a systematic and a perfect manager. There was no doubt in a very short time as to the nature of the disease. It was typhoid fever, the cause probably being the impure water drunk as we were coming home. I have no mind to describe what Ellen suffered. Suffice it to say, that her treatment was soon reduced to watching her every minute night and day, and administering small quantities of milk. Her prostration and emaciation were excessive, and without the most constant attention she might at any moment have slipped out of our hands. I was like a man shipwrecked and alone in a polar country, whose existence depends upon one spark of fire, which he tries to cherish, left glimmering in a handful of ashes. Oh those days, prolonged to weeks, during which that dreadful struggle lasted--days swallowed up with one sole, intense, hungry desire that her life might be spared!--days filled with a forecast of the blackness and despair before me if she should depart. I tried to obtain release from the office. The answer was that nobody could of course prevent my being away, but that it was not usual for a clerk to be absent merely because his wife was not well. The brute added with a sneer that a wife was "a luxury" which he should have thought I could hardly afford. We divided between us, however, at home the twenty-four hours during which we stood sentinels against death, and occasionally we were relieved by one or two friends. I went on duty from about eight in the evening till one in the morning, and was then relieved by Mrs. Taylor, who remained till ten or eleven. She then went to bed, and was replaced by little Marie. What a change came over that child! I was amazed at her. All at once she seemed to have found what she was born to do. The key had been discovered, which unlocked and revealed what there was in her, of which hitherto I had been altogether unaware. Although she was so little, she became a perfect nurse. Her levity disappeared; she was grave as a matron, moved about as if shod in felt, never forgot a single direction, and gave proper and womanly answers to strangers who called. Faculties unsuspected grew almost to full height in a single day. Never did she relax during the whole of that dreadful time, or show the slightest sign of discontent. She sat by her mother's side, intent, vigilant; and she had her little dinner prepared and taken up into the sickroom by Mrs. Taylor before she went to bed. I remember once going to her cot in the night, as she lay asleep, and almost breaking my heart over her with remorse and thankfulness--remorse, that I, with blundering stupidity, had judged her so superficially; and thankfulness, that it had pleased God to present to me so much of His own divinest grace. Fool that I was, not to be aware that messages from Him are not to be read through the envelope in which they are enclosed. I never should have believed, if it had not been for Marie, that any grown-up man could so love a child. Such love, I should have said, was only possible between man and woman, or, perhaps, between man and man. But now I doubt whether a love of that particular kind could be felt towards any grown-up human being, love so pure, so imperious, so awful. My love to Marie was love of God Himself as He is--an unrestrained adoration of an efflux from Him, adoration transfigured into love, because the revelation had clothed itself with a child's form. It was, as I say, the love of God as He is. It was not necessary, as it so often is necessary, to qualify, to subtract, to consider the other side, to deplore the obscurity or the earthly contamination with which the Word is delivered to us. This was the Word itself, without even consciousness on the part of the instrument selected for its vocalisation. I may appear extravagant, but I can only put down what I felt and still feel. I appeal, moreover, to Jesus Himself for justification. I had seen the kingdom of God through a little child. I, in fact, have done nothing more than beat out over a page in my own words what passed through His mind when He called a little child and set him in the midst of His disciples. How I see the meaning of those words now! and so it is that a text will be with us for half a lifetime, recognised as great and good, but not penetrated till the experience comes round to us in which it was born.

Six weeks passed before the faint blue point of light which flickered on the wick began to turn white and show some strength. At last, however, day by day, we marked a slight accession of vitality which increased with change of diet. Every evening when I came home I was gladdened by the tidings which showed advance, and Ellen, I believe, was as much pleased to see how others rejoiced over her recovery as she was pleased for her own sake. She, too, was one of those creatures who always generously admit improvement. For my own part, I have often noticed that when I have been ill, and have been getting better, I have refused to acknowledge it, and that it has been an effort to me to say that things were not at their worst. She, however, had none of this niggardly baseness, and always, if only for the sake of her friends, took the cheerful side. Mrs. Taylor now left us. She left us a friend whose friendship will last, I hope, as long as life lasts. She had seen all our troubles and our poverty: we knew that she knew all about us: she had helped us with the most precious help--what more was there necessary to knit her to us?--and it is worth noting that the assistance which she rendered, and her noble self-sacrifice, so far from putting us, in her opinion, in her debt, only seemed to her a reason why she should be more deeply attached to us.

It was late in the autumn before Ellen had thoroughly recovered, but at last we said that she was as strong as she was before, and we determined to celebrate our deliverance by one more holiday before the cold weather came. It was again Sunday--a perfectly still, warm, autumnal day, with a high barometer and the gentlest of airs from the west. The morning in London was foggy, so much so that we doubted at first whether we should go; but my long experience of London fog told me that we should escape from it with that wind if we got to the chalk downs away out by Letherhead and Guildford. We took the early train to a point at the base of the hills, and wound our way up into the woods at the top. We were beyond the smoke, which rested like a low black cloud over the city in the north-east, reaching a third of the way up to the zenith. The beech had changed colour, and glowed with reddish-brown fire. We sat down on a floor made of the leaves of last year. At mid-day the stillness was profound, broken only by the softest of whispers descending from the great trees which spread over us their protecting arms. Every now and then it died down almost to nothing, and then slowly swelled and died again, as if the Gods of the place were engaged in divine and harmonious talk. By moving a little towards the external edge of our canopy we beheld the plain all spread out before us, bounded by the heights of Sussex and Hampshire. It was veiled with the most tender blue, and above it was spread a sky which was white on the horizon and deepened by degrees into azure over our heads. The exhilaration of the air satisfied Marie, although she had no playmate, and there was nothing special with which she could amuse herself. She wandered about looking for flowers and ferns, and was content. We were all completely happy. We strained our eyes to see the furthest point before us, and we tried to find it on the map we had brought with us. The season of the year, which is usually supposed to make men pensive, had no such effect upon us. Everything in the future, even the winter in London, was painted by Hope, and the death of the summer brought no sadness. Rather did summer dying in such fashion fill our hearts with repose, and even more than repose--with actual joy.

Here ends the autobiography. A month after this last holiday my friend was dead and buried. He had unsuspected disease of the heart, and one day his master, of whom we have heard something, was more than usually violent. Mark, as his custom was, was silent, but evidently greatly excited. His tyrant left the room; and in a few minutes afterwards Mark was seen to turn white and fall forward in his chair. It was all over! His body was taken to a hospital and thence sent home. The next morning his salary up to the day of his death came in an envelope to his widow, without a single word from his employers save a request for acknowledgment. Towards mid-day, his office coat, and a book found in his drawer, arrived in a brown paper parcel, carriage unpaid.

On looking over his papers, I found the sketch of his life and a mass of odds and ends, some apparently written for publication. Many of these had evidently been in envelopes, and had most likely, therefore, been offered to editors or publishers, but all, I am sure, had been refused. I add one or two by way of appendix, and hope they will be thought worth saving.

R. S.

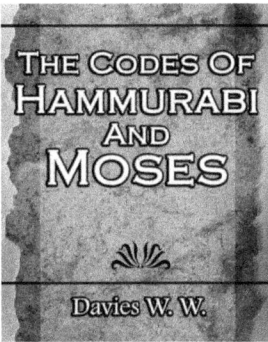

The Codes Of Hammurabi And Moses
W. W. Davies

QTY

The discovery of the Hammurabi Code is one of the greatest achievements of archaeology, and is of paramount interest, not only to the student of the Bible, but also to all those interested in ancient history...

Religion   **ISBN: *1-59462-338-4***   **Pages:132**
MSRP $12.95

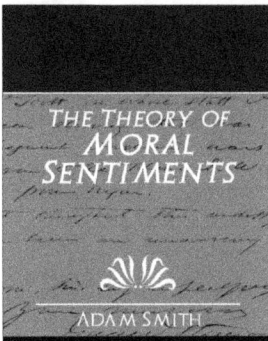

The Theory of Moral Sentiments
Adam Smith

QTY

This work from 1749. contains original theories of conscience amd moral judgment and it is the foundation for systemof morals.

Philosophy ISBN: *1-59462-777-0*   **Pages:536**
MSRP $19.95

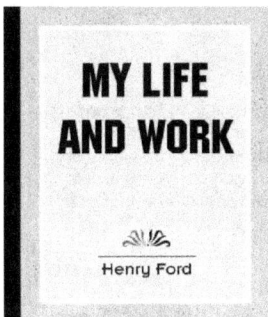

Jessica's First Prayer
Hesba Stretton

QTY

In a screened and secluded corner of one of the many railway-bridges which span the streets of London there could be seen a few years ago, from five o'clock every morning until half past eight, a tidily set-out coffee-stall, consisting of a trestle and board, upon which stood two large tin cans, with a small fire of charcoal burning under each so as to keep the coffee boiling during the early hours of the morning when the work-people were thronging into the city on their way to their daily toil...

Pages:84

Childrens ISBN: *1-59462-373-2*   *MSRP $9.95*

My Life and Work
Henry Ford

QTY

Henry Ford revolutionized the world with his implementation of mass production for the Model T automobile. Gain valuable business insight into his life and work with his own auto-biography... "We have only started on our development of our country we have not as yet, with all our talk of wonderful progress, done more than scratch the surface. The progress has been wonderful enough but..."

Pages:300

Biographies/ ISBN: *1-59462-198-5*   *MSRP $21.95*

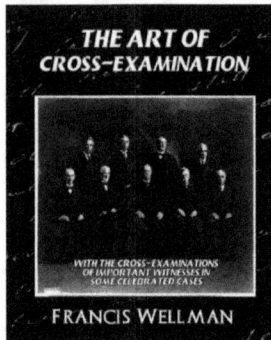

The Art of Cross-Examination
Francis Wellman

QTY

I presume it is the experience of every author, after his first book is published upon an important subject, to be almost overwhelmed with a wealth of ideas and illustrations which could readily have been included in his book, and which to his own mind, at least, seem to make a second edition inevitable. Such certainly was the case with me; and when the first edition had reached its sixth impression in five months, I rejoiced to learn that it seemed to my publishers that the book had met with a sufficiently favorable reception to justify a second and considerably enlarged edition. ..

Pages:412

Reference   ISBN: *1-59462-647-2*   *MSRP $19.95*

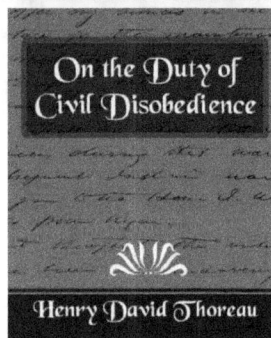

On the Duty of Civil Disobedience
Henry David Thoreau

QTY

Thoreau wrote his famous essay, On the Duty of Civil Disobedience, as a protest against an unjust but popular war and the immoral but popular institution of slave-owning. He did more than write—he declined to pay his taxes, and was hauled off to gaol in consequence. Who can say how much this refusal of his hastened the end of the war and of slavery ?

Law   ISBN: *1-59462-747-9*   **Pages:48**

MSRP $7.45

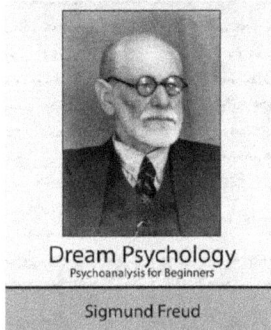

Dream Psychology Psychoanalysis for Beginners
Sigmund Freud

QTY

Sigmund Freud, born Sigismund Schlomo Freud (May 6, 1856 - September 23, 1939), was a Jewish-Austrian neurologist and psychiatrist who co-founded the psychoanalytic school of psychology. Freud is best known for his theories of the unconscious mind, especially involving the mechanism of repression; his redefinition of sexual desire as mobile and directed towards a wide variety of objects; and his therapeutic techniques, especially his understanding of transference in the therapeutic relationship and the presumed value of dreams as sources of insight into unconscious desires.

Pages:196

Psychology   ISBN: *1-59462-905-6*   *MSRP $15.45*

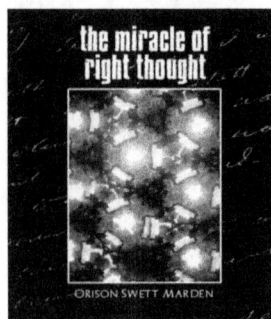

The Miracle of Right Thought
Orison Swett Marden

QTY

Believe with all of your heart that you will do what you were made to do. When the mind has once formed the habit of holding cheerful, happy, prosperous pictures, it will not be easy to form the opposite habit. It does not matter how improbable or how far away this realization may see, or how dark the prospects may be, if we visualize them as best we can, as vividly as possible, hold tenaciously to them and vigorously struggle to attain them, they will gradually become actualized, realized in the life. But a desire, a longing without endeavor, a yearning abandoned or held indifferently will vanish without realization.

Pages:360

Self Help   ISBN: *1-59462-644-8*   *MSRP $25.45*

QTY

The Rosicrucian Cosmo-Conception Mystic Christianity *by Max Heindel* ISBN: *1-59462-188-8* **$38.95**
The Rosicrucian Cosmo-conception is not dogmatic, neither does it appeal to any other authority than the reason of the student. It is: not controversial, but is: sent forth in the, hope that it may help to clear... New Age/Religion Pages 646

Abandonment To Divine Providence *by Jean-Pierre de Caussade* ISBN: *1-59462-228-0* **$25.95**
"The Rev. Jean Pierre de Caussade was one of the most remarkable spiritual writers of the Society of Jesus in France in the 18th Century. His death took place at Toulouse in 1751. His works have gone through many editions and have been republished... Inspirational/Religion Pages 400

Mental Chemistry *by Charles Haanel* ISBN: *1-59462-192-6* **$23.95**
Mental Chemistry allows the change of material conditions by combining and appropriately utilizing the power of the mind. Much like applied chemistry creates something new and unique out of careful combinations of chemicals the mastery of mental chemistry... New Age Pages 354

The Letters of Robert Browning and Elizabeth Barret Barrett 1845-1846 vol II ISBN: *1-59462-193-4* **$35.95**
by Robert Browning and Elizabeth Barrett Biographies Pages 596

Gleanings In Genesis (volume I) *by Arthur W. Pink* ISBN: *1-59462-130-6* **$27.45**
Appropriately has Genesis been termed "the seed plot of the Bible" for in it we have, in germ form, almost all of the great doctrines which are afterwards fully developed in the books of Scripture which follow... Religion/Inspirational Pages 420

The Master Key *by L. W. de Laurence* ISBN: *1-59462-001-6* **$30.95**
In no branch of human knowledge has there been a more lively increase of the spirit of research during the past few years than in the study of Psychology, Concentration and Mental Discipline. The requests for authentic lessons in Thought Control, Mental Discipline and... New Age/Business Pages 422

The Lesser Key Of Solomon Goetia *by L. W. de Laurence* ISBN: *1-59462-092-X* **$9.95**
This translation of the first book of the "Lernegton" which is now for the first time made accessible to students of Talismanic Magic was done, after careful collation and edition, from numerous Ancient Manuscripts in Hebrew, Latin, and French... New Age/Occult Pages 92

Rubaiyat Of Omar Khayyam *by Edward Fitzgerald* ISBN:*1-59462-332-5* **$13.95**
Edward Fitzgerald, whom the world has already learned, in spite of his own efforts to remain within the shadow of anonymity, to look upon as one of the rarest poets of the century, was born at Bredfield, in Suffolk, on the 31st of March, 1809. He was the third son of John Purcell... Music Pages 172

Ancient Law *by Henry Maine* ISBN: *1-59462-128-4* **$29.95**
The chief object of the following pages is to indicate some of the earliest ideas of mankind, as they are reflected in Ancient Law, and to point out the relation of those ideas to modern thought. Religiom/History Pages 452

Far-Away Stories *by William J. Locke* ISBN: *1-59462-129-2* **$19.45**
"Good wine needs no bush," but a collection of mixed vintages does. And this book is just such a collection. Some of the stories I do not want to remain buried for ever in the museum files of dead magazine-numbers an author's not unpardonable vanity..." Fiction Pages 272

Life of David Crockett *by David Crockett* ISBN: *1-59462-250-7* **$27.45**
"Colonel David Crockett was one of the most remarkable men of the times in which he lived. Born in humble life, but gifted with a strong will, an indomitable courage, and unremitting perseverance... Biographies/New Age Pages 424

Lip-Reading *by Edward Nitchie* ISBN: *1-59462-206-X* **$25.95**
Edward B. Nitchie, founder of the New York School for the Hard of Hearing, now the Nitchie School of Lip-Reading, Inc, wrote "LIP-READING Principles and Practice". The development and perfecting of this meritorious work on lip-reading was an undertaking... How-to Pages 400

A Handbook of Suggestive Therapeutics, Applied Hypnotism, Psychic Science ISBN: *1-59462-214-0* **$24.95**
by Henry Munro Health/New Age/Health/Self-help Pages 376

A Doll's House: and Two Other Plays *by Henrik Ibsen* ISBN: *1-59462-112-8* **$19.95**
Henrik Ibsen created this classic when in revolutionary 1848 Rome. Introducing some striking concepts in playwriting for the realist genre, this play has been studied the world over. Fiction/Classics/Plays 308

The Light of Asia *by sir Edwin Arnold* ISBN: *1-59462-204-3* **$13.95**
In this poetic masterpiece, Edwin Arnold describes the life and teachings of Buddha. The man who was to become known as Buddha to the world was born as Prince Gautama of India but he rejected the worldly riches and abandoned the reigns of power when... Religion/History/Biographies Pages 170

The Complete Works of Guy de Maupassant *by Guy de Maupassant* ISBN: *1-59462-157-8* **$16.95**
"For days and days, nights and nights, I had dreamed of that first kiss which was to consecrate our engagement, and I knew not on what spot I should put my lips..." Fiction/Classics Pages 240

The Art of Cross-Examination *by Francis L. Wellman* ISBN: *1-59462-309-0* **$26.95**
Written by a renowned trial lawyer, Wellman imparts his experience and uses case studies to explain how to use psychology to extract desired information through questioning. How-to/Science/Reference Pages 408

Answered or Unanswered? *by Louisa Vaughan* ISBN: *1-59462-248-5* **$10.95**
Miracles of Faith in China Religion Pages 112

The Edinburgh Lectures on Mental Science (1909) *by Thomas* ISBN: *1-59462-008-3* **$11.95**
This book contains the substance of a course of lectures recently given by the writer in the Queen Street Hail, Edinburgh. Its purpose is to indicate the Natural Principles governing the relation between Mental Action and Material Conditions... New Age/Psychology Pages 148

Ayesha *by H. Rider Haggard* ISBN: *1-59462-301-5* **$24.95**
Verily and indeed it is the unexpected that happens! Probably if there was one person upon the earth from whom the Editor of this, and of a certain previous history, did not expect to hear again... Classics Pages 380

Ayala's Angel *by Anthony Trollope* ISBN: *1-59462-352-X* **$29.95**
The two girls were both pretty, but Lucy who was twenty-one who supposed to be simple and comparatively unattractive, whereas Ayala was credited, as her Bombwhat romantic name might show, with poetic charm and a taste for romance. Ayala when her father died was nineteen... Fiction Pages 484

The American Commonwealth *by James Bryce* ISBN: *1-59462-286-8* **$34.45**
An interpretation of American democratic political theory. It examines political mechanics and society from the perspective of Scotsman James Bryce Politics Pages 572

Stories of the Pilgrims *by Margaret P. Pumphrey* ISBN: *1-59462-116-0* **$17.95**
This book explores pilgrims religious oppression in England as well as their escape to Holland and eventual crossing to America on the Mayflower, and their early days in New England... History Pages 268

QTY

The Fasting Cure *by Sinclair Upton*　　　　　　ISBN: *1-59462-222-1*　**$13.95**
*In the Cosmopolitan Magazine for May, 1910, and in the Contemporary Review (London) for April, 1910, I published an article dealing with my experi-
ences in fasting. I have written a great many magazine articles, but never one which attracted so much attention... New Age/Self Help/Health Pages 164*

Hebrew Astrology *by Sepharial*　　　　　　ISBN: *1-59462-308-2*　**$13.45**
*In these days of advanced thinking it is a matter of common observation that we have left many of the old landmarks behind and that we are now pressing
forward to greater heights and to a wider horizon than that which represented the mind-content of our progenitors...　Astrology Pages 144*

Thought Vibration or The Law of Attraction in the Thought World　　ISBN: *1-59462-127-6*　**$12.95**
by William Walker Atkinson　　　　　　　　Psychology/Religion Pages 144

Optimism *by Helen Keller*　　　　　　ISBN: *1-59462-108-X*　**$15.95**
*Helen Keller was blind, deaf, and mute since 19 months old, yet famously learned how to overcome these handicaps, communicate with the world, and
spread her lectures promoting optimism. An inspiring read for everyone...　Biographies/Inspirational Pages 84*

Sara Crewe *by Frances Burnett*　　　　　　ISBN: *1-59462-360-0*　**$9.45**
*In the first place, Miss Minchin lived in London. Her home was a large, dull, tall one, in a large, dull square, where all the houses were alike, and all the
sparrows were alike, and where all the door-knockers made the same heavy sound...　Childrens/Classic Pages 88*

The Autobiography of Benjamin Franklin *by Benjamin Franklin*　　ISBN: *1-59462-135-7*　**$24.95**
*The Autobiography of Benjamin Franklin has probably been more extensively read than any other American historical work, and no other book of its kind
has had such ups and downs of fortune. Franklin lived for many years in England, where he was agent...　Biographies/History Pages 332*

Name	
Email	
Telephone	
Address	
City, State ZIP	

☐ **Credit Card**　　　　☐ **Check / Money Order**

Credit Card Number	
Expiration Date	
Signature	

*Please Mail to:　Book Jungle
PO Box 2226
Champaign, IL 61825
or Fax to:　　630-214-0564*

ORDERING INFORMATION
web: *www.bookjungle.com*
email: *sales@bookjungle.com*
fax: *630-214-0564*
mail: *Book Jungle PO Box 2226 Champaign, IL 61825*
or PayPal *to sales@bookjungle.com*

Please contact us for bulk discounts

DIRECT-ORDER TERMS

**20% Discount if You Order
Two or More Books**
Free Domestic Shipping!
Accepted: Master Card, Visa,
Discover, American Express

www.ingramcontent.com/pod-product-compliance
Lightning Source LLC
LaVergne TN
LVHW081325060426
835511LV00011B/1857